Design
for
Human
Scale

Design
for
Human
Scale

Victor Papanek

VAN NOSTRAND REINHOLD COMPANY
NEW YORK   CINCINNATI   TORONTO   LONDON   MELBOURNE

Copyright © 1983 by Van Nostrand Reinhold Company Inc.
Library of Congress Catalog Card Number 82-21906
ISBN 0-442-27616-8

Printed in the United States of America
Designed by Ben Kann

Published by Van Nostrand Reinhold Company Inc.
135 West 50th Street
New York, New York 10020

Van Nostrand Reinhold
480 Latrobe Street
Melbourne, Victoria 3000, Australia

Van Nostrand Reinhold Company Limited
Molly Millars Lane
Wokingham, Berkshire, England   RG11 2PY

16 15 14 13 12 11 10 9 8 7 6 5 4 3 2 1

Library of Congress Cataloging in Publication Data

Papanek, Victor
    Design for human scale.

    Bibliography: p.
    Includes index.
    1. Design.   I. Title.   2. Architecture.   3. Sociology.
NK1510.P27   1983   745.4   82-21906
ISBN 0-442-27616-8

Acknowledgments

DURING the five years I spent developing the thoughts that eventually led to this book, I have consciously rejected grants, stipends, government support, or any other financial aid from academic, national or international organizations. But my design work and lectures made it possible for me to spend a number of years living and working in northern Europe and Australia. Extended time periods spent in Malaysia; Nigeria; Papua, New Guinea; India; and Brazil helped me to view *Design for Human Scale* from a global perspective.

I feel I should thank many friends with whom I discussed much of the material in this book. Claudia Brandão Mattos, a young industrial and graphic designer from Rio de Janeiro, spent many long days and nights in passionate discussion with me. She brought a sense of freshness to my thinking about design and could always be depended upon to ask difficult questions and tenaciously batter away until we found an answer. She also opened my eyes to the design, popular arts, and the countryside of Brazil; my lectures at the National Catholic University of Rio de Janeiro served as a sort of dress rehearsal for this book. Cědo Keller, a designer and professor from Zagreb, taught me much by exposing me to designers and students in Yugoslavia on half a dozen visits to that country. He also sharpened my insight through long debates about the role of design, while together we visited Mexico, Ireland, India, Germany, and Belgium. Brett Iggulden of Bellingen in Australia gave me the opportunity to design for his firm; with his wife Prue he provided good wine, heated discussions, flights in a sailplane, and warm love.

Uffe Skeppstedt and his wife Jannicke, Nordal Åkerman and Pelle Johansson, all from Sweden spent many long evenings with me passionately arguing about the relationship between people and design. In England I was able to enlarge my insight through talks with Peter Bone, Paul Callaghan, Patrick Wallis Burke, and Mark Brutton. Christel and Christer Holmgren and Jan Trägårdh of Denmark; Carl Auböck and Harald Kubelka of Vienna and Al Gowan from Boston; all provided the sort of intellectual environment that made it possible for me to test my thinking. Special thanks need to be expressed to fellow members in the International Congress of Societies of Industrial Design's Developing Countries Design Information Group: Paul Hogan from the Republic of Ireland and my good friend Knut Yran (former Vice-President of Design of Philips, Eindhoven).

Finally I must thank my two editors, Kate Manasian and Jenny Towndrow, both in London, for helping me make this book say what I wanted with precision and grace.

Contents

For
Claudia Brandão Mattos *of Brazil*
Goroslav (Cĕdo) Keller *of Yugoslavia*
Brett Iggulden *of Australia*

The existence of things is profitable,
The non-existence of things is serviceable.
LAO-TZÛ

All we have is our Hands
And a hole in God's Earth.
FEDERICO GARCIA LORCA

Introduction

THE tools we use; the spaces in which we live and work; the vehicles we drive or ride or fly; the means we use to communicate, listen to music, or watch television; the artifacts we fashion to become symbols, impart delight, use in sports, teach, or assert status—all of these are products of design and architecture.

This quest for fitness of form, purpose, and beauty allied in one meaningful whole is a joyous activity; it combines creative, intellectual ventures with intuitive, playful elements. To create a home, design a chair, fashion a cooling vessel, develop sound-reproduction equipment, make a better bicycle, or help plan a village—is a joyful adventure. At the most basic level, design and architecture are activities that affirm life. By bringing order

1

and meaning to chaos, the designer holds back the dark entropic forces of anarchic disarray that often make our lives seem pointless and our efforts random.

Design is the innate pattern-making impulse of human beings. Design and architecture are the tools mankind uses to change and adapt to its environment, extend human capacities, and thus comprehensively change itself.

Architecture has been defined as "the art or science of building or constructing edifices of any kind *for human use.*" [italics supplied] "*. . . but Architecture is sometimes regarded as a fine art, and then has a narrower meaning.*"[1]

We can all think of architecture that enchants us: an unplanned alpine village nestled around an apricot-colored church in a remote Austrian valley; the low, dun, saurian shapes of a pueblo near Santa Fe; the crazy quilt of rice terraces and huts marching down the Bedugal mountainside on the island of Bali; or the quiet beauty of Katsura Palace in the Japanese moonlight.

But it is not only the anonymous past that brings us enchantment. We can find recent examples in the architecture of Frank Lloyd Wright; in Hassam Fathy's hand-built villages in Nubia and southern Egypt; in Herb Greene's houses, creeping like the shingled exoskeletons of fabled insects across the plains of Oklahoma, and in Alvar Aalto's Villa Mairea; a sleeping beauty in the birch forests of Finland. The kinship between these homes is their concern for human use and enjoyment.

In design, we can also find many examples where visual delight, sensitive choice of materials, and fitness for use are clearly expressed: the austere shapes beloved by the potters of the Sung dynasty; the knifelike prow of a Viking ship slicing through deep blue water; a single joint of bamboo sliced into a ceremonial tea whisk by Kyoto craftsmen a thousand years ago (figure I-1); the clean lines of a modern American racing sulky (figure I-2); and the simple and elegant severity of Shaker furniture (figure I-3).

Today we can find delight in chairs and tables from Finland and Denmark, in the subtle harmonies of British tweeds, and in the sleek and dependable precision of German and Japanese cameras. We value the reliability of a Permobil wheelchair from Sweden (figure I-4); a surgical lamp from Australia; tents, back-

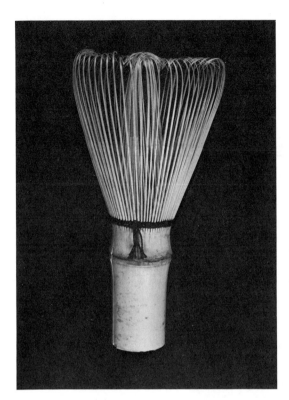

Figure I-1. *Bamboo ceremonial tea whisk from Japan. Author's collection. (Photograph by John Charlton)*

Figure I-2. *American racing sulky. (Photograph courtesy of Hughes Studio and the Houghton Sulky Co., Marion, Ohio)*

3

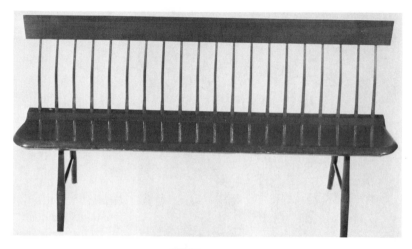

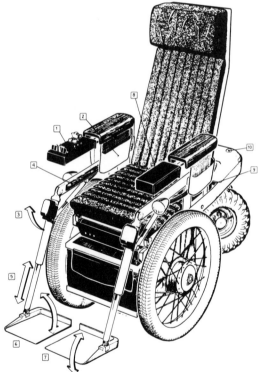

Figure I-3. *Meeting-house bench made in a Shaker community between 1855 and 1865.* (Photograph courtesy of Collections of Greenfield Village and the Henry Fovel Museum, Dearborn, Michigan Negative No. 851124)

Figure I-4. *Permobil motorized wheelchair.* (Photograph courtesy of Permobil, Sweden and Saab, Sweden)

packs, and sleeping bags from the United States; or a superbly designed and engineered computer. A hand-held translation machine with several different language modules adds convenience to travel, as does the breathtakingly lucid shape of the Concorde SST. We are pleased and astonished at designs incorporating microminiaturized chip technology in teaching machines, calculators, and diagnostic devices in medicine.

Yet something has gone wrong.

From New York to Novosibirsk, Tokyo to Toronto, London to Lima, and Penang to Paris, architects have dehumanized our cities by erecting anonymous high-rise structures that destroy any sense of territoriality. People find themselves tucked away in giant filing cabinets in vast dormitory towns at night, only to occupy startlingly similar glassy beehives as their work spaces. For extreme examples of this we only have to mention Pruitt-Igoe. This enormous public housing complex in St. Louis, Missouri, which won awards for its "sensitive" design, proved so alienating to its residents that only eighteen years after it was built the city government was forced to dynamite some of the buildings to stop the murder, rape, and juvenile delinquency.

Design and architecture have all too often ignored people's real needs. Mass production has turned many manufacturers into latter day sorcerer's apprentices—unaware at the way a small misjudgement, multiplied a million times or more, can tatter social coherence.

In 1979, nearly one third of the automobiles manufactured in the United States were recalled because inherent design faults and engineering mistakes threatened life and safety.[2] We curse the appliances and gadgets that clutter our lives and that seem to wear out at nearly the same rate as the warranty. We struggle to our garbage cans staggering under our national average of eighty-six cubic feet of empty boxes, wrappers, milk cartons, and nonreturnable bottles and egg boxes, all lovingly compacted into enormous plastic bags. Our garages are filled with broken dishwashers, three-year-old television sets, coffee percolators discarded for later models, malfunctioning pop-up toasters, and cameras we stopped using. Not only are these habits wasteful, they are no longer acceptable when unemployment is high, energy and raw materials are in limited supply, and many people in the southern half of the globe are dying from starvation.

What has gone wrong? Many architects and designers have become "artistic" in the late capitalist sense of the word. That is, a continuing escalation of difference for difference's sake in a vain attempt to shock the no longer shockable bourgeoisie. A recent show of contemporary designers' chairs from Italy presented twenty-five chairs, yet only two were strong enough to support the weight of a person comfortably.[3] Clearly, the designers were no longer developing chairs, but exhibition pieces totally unrelated to human needs. Architects have also resolutely turned their backs on human need, providing us with "conceptual" buildings and post-modern eccentricities. Like Herman Hesse's bead game in *Magister Ludi*, much design and architecture is now a game played by an increasingly small elite, with a complete disregard for people.

Social critics, aestheticians, critics, designers, architects, and consumers are all trying to determine the cause of the problem.[4] With jejune simplicity, they try to find the *one* factor responsible. The lack of usability in products, as well as their lack of aesthetics, has been blamed at various times on egocentric designers, un-motivated workers, greedy manufacturers, passive consumers, abrasive advertisers, and unscrupulous marketing people. But the answer is a good deal more complex.

It is certainly possible to blame aggressive, sometimes belligerent mass-media advertising that encourages people to buy things they neither need nor want. High-pressure marketing also persuades people to accept things uncritically, without looking for quality and high standards of workmanship.

A mass production society generates the technology most effective for mass scale. This can create some curious paradoxes such as the fact that an automobile purchased for $10,000, which is well cared for, inspected, and reasonably maintained, may rust in five to eight years, while a beer can carelessly tossed into the bushes may remain flawless for twenty or thirty years.

The basic problem with design today lies not with design (and certainly not with marketing, manufacturing, or quality control), but with the relationship between design and people, or rather, the *lack* of a relationship between design and people. Two new areas must be considered by designers: alternative means of distribution, and the consequences of the design act itself.

To develop a design that will solve a problem on many different levels is one way of decentralizing the means of production and, at the same time, making more choices available to users of the design. As will be shown later, it is possible to solve a design problem so that the resulting product can be made at the mass-production, individual-kit, village- and cottage-industry levels, and by other hybrid production methods yet undreamed of. To include people more directly is a new consideration for designers.

The ways in which a new product, tool, artifact, or building can change people and society, do harm to a fragile culture, destroy ecological balances or enrich us all through energy savings is a second consideration for designers.

These two new considerations compelled me to write this book.

Years ago, when I first began working in Denmark, I was shown a diagram in which the words *design, engineering, marketing,* and *people* were arranged around a cross (figure I-5). I was told design begins with designers, is engineered down to earth, marketed, and then given to the people. This concept is wrong. Design should not begin with designers, but with people. People—consumers or end users—and designers must determine the direction of design together.

A new diagram is offered (figure I-6). Note that it now has sixteen spokes instead of four and that design now begins with people. The process goes through design analysis and engineering phases and is subjected to design research, which looks Janus-like at both the past and the future.

A biological design approach can provide solutions to problems by translating a natural, organic design or system into a man-made system or object, so that it operates analogous to nature. It can also provide a diagnosis of design faults [see my study, (56) in the Bibliography]. Biomorphic design, biomechanics, and bionics are of course closely linked to the environment and ecology. I devoted an entire chapter to this approach in *Design for the Real World* more than a decade ago).[5] Specifically, biomorphic design means searching for a solution or an analog to a solution in biology, and then using that solution to help solve a design problem.

For example, it has been known for hundreds of years that it

7

Figure I-5. *Basic flowchart explaining the design process, as used by the Department of Industrial Design, Royal Academy of Architecture, Copenhagen.*

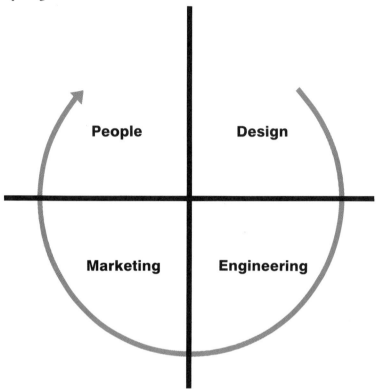

is possible to get an exact reading of ambient temperature by counting the number of chirps per minute of a katydid, multiplying it by 20 and then dividing by 160.

To establish how a katydid tells temperature may help us to understand how things work and may lead to solutions to design problems which otherwise would go unsolved.[6] Biology consequently fills one of the new areas in our redesigned diagram.

A study of how other societies and cultures have dealt with a design problem can also give a designer new orientation. Housing and villages in eastern and western Africa that reflect kinship and friendship structures could make an important contribution to western architecture and planning, altering the profound rigidity of previous architectural modes of thought. Therefore social anthropology and history also form new spokes in the diagram.

Figure I-6. *The improved flowchart, note the many spaces that are still open for future expansion. Author's design, Copenhagen, 1973.*

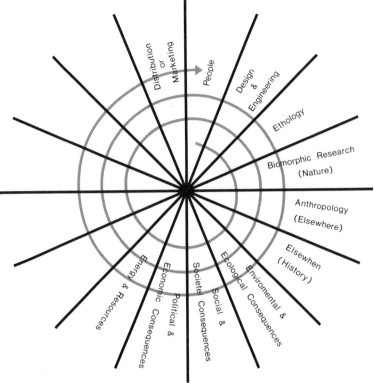

But since design also looks to the future and to the ramifications design might usher in, these consequences appear as new spokes as well. Distribution, implying both conventional and alternative marketing methods, continue the diagram's flow.

It will be seen that there are still many empty spokes. They are to be filled in when we know more about design. Just as biomorphic design did not exist as a serious design consideration until I introduced it in 1953 (leaning heavily on German and French discoveries in bionics), so other approaches, as yet untried, may one day become important elements in the design process.

Ecological and environmental concerns have always affected life and have emerged in academic disciplines during the last fifty years. When *Design for the Real World* was written fifteen years ago, concern for the environment on the part of the designer and involvement with ecology and ethology by architects and designers

9

was still considered radical. Now these new areas have a place. In five, ten, or fifty years, designers and architects will not only be able to fill in the remaining empty slots, but will probably have to enlarge the diagram.

One more important point. In the first diagram the flow was a single arc, beginning with "design" and ending with "impacting" on people. The second diagram is a spiral, *beginning with people* and curving like a helix through all the sections, repeating its motion continually. Instead of one single turn, the helix repeats again and again, gathering more and more feedback.

Industrial designers, industry and government should examine together the social and ecological harm being done to our communities by the waste of energy and resources and by chemical and noise pollution. To blame the mess on a profit-seeking capitalist system is silly; our friends in socialist states have the same problems.

To say that technology itself is wrong might lead to the elimination of the only weapon we have, producing a world-wide crisis. Through multinational corporations, "assistance" programs from the USA, USSR, and China, most third world countries have been forced into great dependence on technology. Developing nations depend on modern technology for food storage, water purification, birth control, health care, and manufacturing methods. The impact of such a crisis would be felt there first (as can be seen by the shaky economies of many of these countries due to the energy crisis). If industrial methods are exported without modification from fully industrialized countries to those in the southern half of the globe, there may be far-reaching social, ecological, ethological, and environmental consequences such as pollution and cultural alienation.

In the developed countries we pay for our progress by living with high rates of suicide, vandalism, absenteeism, work sabotage, wildcat strikes, alcoholism, sport violence, child battering, divorce, deviant sexual behavior, drug abuse, loss of identity, and finally *anomie*.

We are all aware of 'pollution through products,' but few of us realize how complex the cycle is

1. Natural resources are destroyed. Often these resources are irreplaceable.

2. The destruction of these resources (i.e., strip mining, open-pit mining) creates pollution.

3. The manufacturing process creates more pollution.

4. Packaging the product destroys more natural resources and creates more pollution.

5. The use of the product creates more pollution, as in the case of cars emitting exhaust fumes.

6. Discarding the product creates another source of pollution.

The intervention of designers must be modest, minimal, and sensitive.

In developing countries, the problems and negative consequences of design intervention that is not *design for human scale* can often be seen more clearly than in the western world.

Thus we find that the indigo-dyeing of textiles in western Africa creates major breeding areas for tsetse flies and anopheles mosquitoes, the answer is not to get rid of the dyeing pits, but to introduce biological controls. If in Lesotho the social life of women is centered around the beating of maize, the answer is not to introduce electric maize-grinding machinery, but to simplify the work and still retain the social grouping.

In *Design for the Real World*, I raised three main points:

1. Most design is carried out for well-to-do, middle class, middle-aged people living in developed societies. Designers have neglected the handicapped, the poor, the retarded, children and babies, the elderly, the obese, and people in developing countries, among others.

2. Design must be carried out by cross-disciplinary and inter-disciplinary teams that include end users and workers.

3. Many design schools and designers work for a fantasy world (luxury hotels on the ocean floor, 3-D television systems, and other resource-wasting trivia) when they should be looking at the real world instead.

The point of *Design for the Real World* can be summed up as: *What to design and why.*

Design for Human Scale carries this question to its next logical step. After deciding on *what* and *why*, the next question is *how?* That is the central question here. How can people be built into the design process? How can designs and people be brought together?

This book shows how people can influence the design of the tools, transportation devices, housing, products, objects, artifacts, and visual messages that form their environment. It also states what designers must do to reestablish a reciprocal flow between people and designers. For too long the design profession has fought consumer input. This book shows through suggestions, hints, and even some "how-to" strategies, what we all can do to create design for human scale.

Ahmedabad (India); *Bellingen, NSW* (Australia); *Rio de Janeiro* (Brazil) *1977–1983.*

1

Broadening Constituencies

It is dangerous to adopt absolute freedom in inventing needs, products, and machines: and in showing such inventions to people in the way of temptation, commercial deception, expenditure, and wide-spread publicity. Lack of consideration and discrimination— even with regard to human medication and agriculture—has rendered contemporary man, producer and consumer, a slave subjected to the creativity of the machine, its purposes, and its diversity of production.

KAMAL JUMBLAT[1]

F OR me, it all began with my mother. She was an unusually short woman, about four feet eleven inches tall. Being so short was quite a handicap. Washing the dishes was enormously difficult for her, since the sink was far too high. Reaching pots, pans, dishes, or glasses in kitchen cabinets and on shelves was equally hard. She experienced these same problems when trying to reach goods that had been placed on the upper shelves of grocery stores and supermarkets.

As far as I was concerned, most of her difficulties arose at home. In 1949, while a design and architecture student, I worked

13

part time in a large New York design office. One evening, finding my boss in a relaxed and rather mellow mood, I told him about some of my mother's problems and asked him if there was anything we, as designers, could do to help.

He leaned back in his chair, roared with laughter, and said, "There are more important things for our office to worry about than helping a few little old ladies."

I went home disturbed. A major difficulty in living and working, which I saw my mother troubled by every day, could apparently not be solved through design. And apart from her, how many other "little old ladies" were there who suffered from the same problem?

I spoke to my professor who recommended that I make a list. I started with the assumption that my mother was far from unique and that there must be other women four feet eleven inches tall. I did not know where to get hard facts, so I just guessed. If my mother was that short, I estimated that there were probably at least 100,000 other little old ladies in North America. (My guess was wrong: the number was nearly half a million according to the U.S. Census Service for 1940, but I would like the reader to follow the same conservative steps I followed more than thirty years ago.)

If there *really* were the 100,000 little old ladies I guessed there were, it stood to reason that there were also approximately 100,000 little old men.

I now had 200,000 short people. Were there any more? World War II had ended less than four years earlier. Hunger and near starvation were widespread in Europe and Asia. Decent nutrition, minerals, and vitamins were lacking in most of the world and this poor diet affected body height directly. Using population statistics relating to human stature of that period, I realized that, with remarkably few exceptions, nearly the entire populations of Asia, Africa, South and Central America, the Middle East, Mexico, Micronesia, the Pacific Islands, and even southern Europe were short and might be added to my list.

I now had 1,500,200,000 people. Were there any more?

All of us are between four and five feet tall at some time between our ninth and eighteenth birthdays, and the number of children in the world in that age group stood at about 250,000,000.

I noted that people in wheelchairs were also shorter than average, but by this time it seemed frivolous to try to compute their number, when the figure I had already reached encompassed nearly seven-eighths of all humanity. It now remained to convince the design establishment that we were trying to help nearly three billion people rather than just a few little old ladies.

Before looking at the design results, let us analyze what was done. I refused to accept an artificial and narrow definition of the needs of a group considered to be "too small for concern." By examining the ways in which this group differed from "normal" people, I found that these differences were shared by many others.

I broadened the constituency that could be helped through design intervention so much that even a profit-oriented manufacturing and marketing concern would pay attention.

The next step was to see if the same problem, or a similar one, had already been solved at some other time, or in some other culture.

The Japanese, for their own comfort, as well as to keep the *tatami* floormats in their homes clean, wear canvas, socklike slippers called *tabi* (figure 1-1). These *tabi* separate the big toe from the rest of the foot. When leaving the house, foot and *tabi* are slipped into wooden thong sandals called *geta* (figure 1-2). *Geta* come in many different heights from five to twenty-five centimeters (figures 1-3 and 1-4). They keep the feet from touching mud or snow. Obviously, after a heavy snowfall, the tallest *geta* are worn.

With this information it was possible to develop *geta*-like footgear that were immediately helpful to my mother (figure 1-5). By developing a clamp-on or step-in device that raised the user's height by nine to twenty-four inches, many chores could be simplified (although made somewhat more precarious). It might be possible to paint the upper parts of wall and ceilings, harvest fruit, and do many other tricky jobs that were normally slightly out of reach.

Having come full circle, I have demonstrated that by *broadening the constituency*, products can be developed that are useful to the remaining "one-eighth" of humanity.

Another example: most of the world uses straight, lever-action door handles but the United States and Canada are known around

Figure 1-1. *Contemporary Japanese* tabi *socks.*

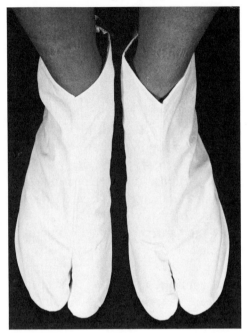

the world as "the countries with round doorknobs." One minority affected by this practice is the 40,000 *myasthenia gravis* sufferers who can turn a round doorknob only with great difficulty, due to the weakness of their muscles.

Now to broaden the constituency. Who else has trouble with round doorknobs? Well, there are people with arthritis, the elderly, and small children. There are those who have lost a hand through disease or accident. There are people in wheelchairs and on crutches. There are those who can work a lever with their cane, crutch, hook, stump, or, in the case of quadraplegics, their chin but who have difficulty grasping and turning a round knob. But before this broadening of constituencies becomes a rallying point for the lame, consider this.

All of us have tried to open a door with wet hands after a shower, after coming in from the rain, or after having just done the dishes. And our hands have probably slipped on those silly round knobs. Try visualizing a young mother, a small child on

Figure 1-2. *Women's and men's wooden* geta *from Japan, designed to keep the wearer's foot above puddles or snow.* (Photograph by John Charlton)

Figure 1-3. *Obviously puddles in Taiwan are even deeper: these farm women's* Muji *are rough but show great vernacular elegance. They are much taller than the Japanese version.* (Photograph by John Charlton)

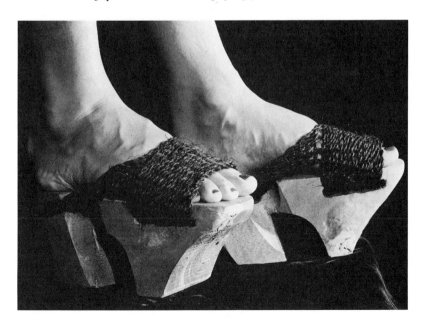

Figure 1-4. *Long ago Japanese* geta *were also quite tall. Detail from a woodcut by Hokusai. Author's collection.*

her hip, with diapers, bottles, handbag, shopping bag, and keys trying to get in the door. We are all loaded down with packages from time to time and round doorknobs just do not make any sense.

From roughly 40,000 people with *myasthenia gravis*, I have again broadened our constituency to include nearly everyone.

How are these problems solved in an actual design practice?

Some years ago when I worked as a restaurant cook, I often had to prepare open-faced sandwiches—hundreds of them. Preparation meant slicing eight sticks of Hungarian salami wafer thin, then doing the same to mortadella, prosciutto, and bread. Like others before me, I developed a strained wrist, what my doctor referred to with savage irony as "tennis elbow." All this started me thinking about others who might suffer from the same problem.

18

Figure 1-5.
Drawing of the geta-like elevated slippers I designed for my mother in 1948.

Although most white bread available in the United States is presliced, some of us prefer to buy whole loaves or bake our own. Slicing a loaf of home-baked bread (or salami or sausage) fatigues the wrist. It is tiring to most people and sheer torture to the old.

There are, of course, gadgets such as rotary slicers that are not only dangerous but take up needed counter space. In addition, they are hard to clean and sharpen, and provide breeding grounds for germs. Their electric equivalents have the same faults, but they cost more, break down more easily, and waste energy.

The problem was to redesign the handle of a slicing knife so that the wrist and elbow of the user were less fatigued, or not tired at all. After designing, building, and testing a number of working prototypes, three solutions on three different levels were found.

The first of these is a standard slicing blade with a highly contoured handle (figure 1-6). The knife comes with a cutting board that provides a guide slit that helps with the slicing. The handle and slicing board are molded plastic and are designed for mass production and commercial distribution in large numbers.

The second version works in precisely the same way, but has been designed for the Southern Appalachian Self-Help Project (figure 1-7). This version provides a slit that serves as a scabbard to store the knife blade.

A third handle was developed specifically for patients in clinics, hospitals, and retirement homes. In this version, the handle is papier-mâché over a wire armature (figure 1-8). It can also be made of a self-forming plastic (like that used on the inside of expensive downhill ski boots). This version can be custom fitted to the hands of individual patients, and can be used by people no longer able to use their wrists.

Wrist efficiency is increased by 30 to 35% with the first two versions, and 85% with the third.

The knife illustrated in figure 1-9 is now being produced by Gustavsberg AB of Sweden and is so successful in reducing wrist fatigue that a meat slicer and frozen food cutter have been added to the range. By *broadening the constituency* from the elderly to all people, Gustavsberg has captured a large part of the home market and secured excellent export sales.

We all know or think we know about the problems of being blind. Watching a blind person feel his way along a street, white cane tapping antennalike; observing a Seeing Eye dog lead his master through busy traffic; seeing a blind person's hand follow the miniature mountainscape of braille across a page. We can

Figure 1-6. *Slicing knife and cutting guide designed by Mike Staley, as a student at the Kansas City Art Institute.*

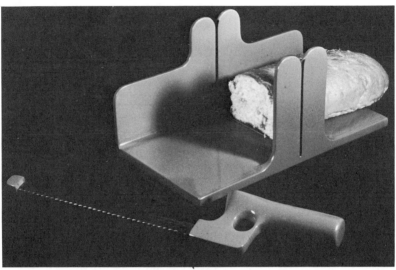

sense the struggle and we may even feel a little of that black recondite prison—a world without butterflies, sunsets, colors, paintings, candlelight, or twinkling stars. But unless we are blind, we can never fully understand.

There is another prison less known and little discussed; the prison of blurred, dark shapes and dim light. The world of low vision: those who are legally blind but can still distinguish large, well-defined shapes in bright light. Their life is one without many books, films, landscapes, television, or remembered faces. Although special "reading" and scanning machines are available, they are unusually expensive and very cumbersome.

Because many of the people afflicted with low vision are elderly, we are talking about a group that is discriminated against twice.

Medical research may someday find the cure that will lighten the burden of low vision sufferers, but design is about the here and now. Simply then, the question for the designer regarding low vision is: how can I help make life pleasanter, or more bearable, for people with this problem?

In 1979, Melissa Duffner, one of my senior students at Kansas City Art Institute, became immersed in the problem of low vision

Figure 1-7. *A different solution, specifically designed for cottage level, handcarved production of the Southern Appalachian Self-Help Project. Note slit in board for knife storage. Designed by James Ross, as a student at the Kansas City Art Institute.*

Figure 1-8. *Knife handle designed to be custom made for each patient's hand in a clinic. Designed by Adrian Lonecker as a student at the Kansas City Art Institute.*

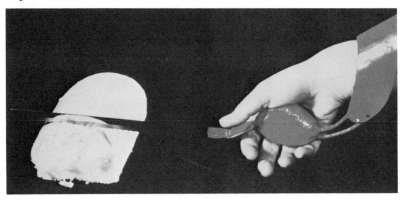

Figure 1-9. *Slicing knife and cutting board with slit. Mass produced by Gustavsberg, A. B., in Sweden. (Photograph courtesy of Gustavsberg, A. B., Sweden)*

for one of her projects. She worked intensively with Dr. Robert Sutton, a victim of low vision.

Dr. Sutton contributed his personal experience and medical background. while Melissa contributed her knowledge of graphic and industrial design. This mixture of aesthetic insight, clinical experience, personal suffering, and disciplined design resulted in a design team well equipped to cope with problems of low vision.

In discussing the difficulties facing low vision sufferers, Dr. Sutton mentioned that one of the pleasures for people suffering from this malady was playing cards. Yet because it was necessary to play with normal card decks, low-vision players were forced to use devices such as strong magnifying glasses in order to participate. Melissa Duffner decided that this was a problem she could solve.

The design team substituted shapes such as circles, squares, and triangles for clubs, hearts, spades, and diamonds. In the center of each shape the traditional symbol was retained to make play between low vision and normally sighted people possible. To avoid confusion, the traditional clubs, hearts, diamonds, and spades were subdued by an 80% screen making them invisible to the partially sighted. These cards were then tested at the Low Vision Clinic of the Truman Medical Center.

Marketing these improved cards at first seemed hopeless—manufacturers of playing cards claimed that no market existed because their own low-vision decks did not sell.

But there was a market. Commercial low-vision cards on sale at the time were badly designed (figure 1-10). One commercial deck was color coded in blue, green, red, and black, confusing the sighted and invisible to those who could barely see.

Student designer and low-vision end user became design entrepreneurs to bring cards and people together. The Low Vision 20/200 cards are now in production and selling well. They are easy to understand, simple to read, well designed, and astonishingly beautiful.

This is one example of how, on a modest human scale, design

Figure 1-10. *Compare the commercially available low-vision cards (top row) with Melissa Duffner's design. Note the confusing images and tortured numerals and letters in the commercial pack. The "A" and the "4" look identical to most people with low vision. The commercial deck's instructions has many lines of fine print to communicate with people that are practically blind. There are no instructions necessary for Melissa Duffner's deck; where to obtain another deck is stated in bold type.*

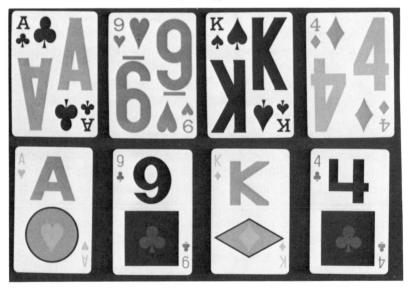

entrepreneurship can solve problems that the high-volume mass production system cannot handle.

The elderly have difficulty finding comfortable chairs that allow good seating posture and are easy to sit down in or get up out of. The relationship between seat and back, seat and arm height, and the weight of the chair are important considerations when attempting to bring comfort to the elderly. Bruno Mathsson of Sweden manufactures a superbly designed and crafted chair with these factors in mind. Made of wood laminate and upholstered in a liquid-resistant, cotton-based fabric, it is handsome and anatomically healthful. But it is expensive and after payment of shipping and import taxes, is out of reach of most retirement homes and elderly people.

Many other chairs for the elderly are manufactured in the United States and Great Britain. These chairs are usually made of chrome steel tubing, a material as cold as a corpse and as unpleasant to touch. The upholstery is usually some vinyl-coated fabric or other plastic-based material. These materials become sticky when they are sat on all day, may lead to skin rashes (similar to bed sores), and can become dangerously slippery. Because the chairs' structures are tubing, they are usually lightweight, meaning that an older person sitting in one and reaching for something can risk a nasty spill.

The job then was to design a chair for the elderly that fitted their needs, was made of forgiving inexpensive materials, and looked humane. One of my students moved into a retirement home. He believed that end users should be part of the design team and that living side by side with the elderly would be the best way of understanding their problems. He lived there for nearly six months observing residents using chairs. He discovered that old people were happy to discuss the problems of sitting down, standing up, and the comfort of chairs in general.

Through his observations the student learned what the elderly used chairs for, how they used them and what special requirements were necessary (because the elderly are often incontinent, a water-resistant fabric was important). He was surprised to learn that one of the most common uses of chairs was as support. He noticed that as elderly residents approached a chair, they often grabbed onto it, sometimes pushing it along the floor with them as they crossed the room. If a chair was not secure enough, it could tip over, causing an accident.

He was also struck by the fact that most of the residents felt irrelevant to society. After sixty-five or seventy years of active living, the triviality of television and shuffleboard were not enough. They sometimes felt humiliated that they were *given* food and a room. They wanted to give back something in return. Some of the men had been cabinetmakers and carpenters during their active lives. With their help and advice, and after testing various ergonomic configurations, the ultimate chair design emerged, the product of designer and end user cooperation. The final chair (figure 1-11), made of wood and a canvaslike transportation cloth, was designed to be built and assembled by some of the elderly

Figure 1-11. *Chair to be made by elderly craftsmen in retirement homes for other elderly people on a custom basis. Designed by Blackman and others as graduate students at Purdue University.*

residents for the others. This decentralized the chair production to the retirement homes and reduced the cost of each chair. More importantly, it put caring and love back into the making of the object itself.

This chapter began with short people. We frequently overlook the fact that children and the elderly are, comparatively speaking, quite short. But even if "normal" (between 5 feet 8 inches and 6 feet 4 inches for the average man), height may change dramatically. Some years ago I had an accident while piloting a glider. This put me in a wheelchair temporarily. Suddenly, instead of my normal 5 feet 8½ inches, I was 4 feet 1 inch tall (a wheelchair is only a car crash, skiing accident, or virus away). Suddenly I could not reach the shelves in a supermarket, get through a door easily, or carry out simple day-to-day tasks.

A major problem with being short as a child or in a wheelchair is reaching a sink. For this reason, it would be extremely convenient if kitchen and bathroom sinks were adjustable in height.

Catering to this very real need, some years ago a division of General Motors unveiled their adjustable sink with all the advertising hoopla conceivable. It was electrohydraulically operated and cost $6,000 to buy and $700 to install. In other words, the two bathrooms and kitchen of a home would cost $20,100 to convert.

In the industrial design department of Leeds Polytechnic in England, the problem was posed of designing the same sink that was simpler and less expensive. Was it possible to design a wall support that would hold a standard kitchen or bathroom sink and that could be easily raised or lowered by hand by children, people in wheelchairs, people on crutches, or the elderly? More importantly, was it possible to use off-the-shelf, existing hardware and reduce the price, including installation, from $6,700 to $67?

Under the guidance of a Professor Hardcastle, a Leeds student did just that (figure 1-12). The assembly was so strong and the operating wheel so easy to use that an arthritic patient in a wheelchair was able to raise and lower the sink support bracket with one hand, even with a 180-pound man standing on it (for testing purposes). Any person adept with his or her hands could build the unit for a friend, relative, or neighbor.

Figure 1-12. *Adjustable sink for the handicapped. Designed by James Gilliland as a student at Leeds College of Art under the guidance of Professor Hardcastle. Patent applied for, 1968.* (Courtesy of Professor Hardcastle, Leeds Polytechnic, England)

Instead of launching yet another product onto the market, the 'product' in this case was an illustrated comic booklike instruction sheet (figure 1-13). All of the parts were available from a hardware store, except the support platform, which could be made from pressed steel (mass produced at about $8 a time), structural foam (mass produced again, at about $14), or marine bonded ¾-inch plywood (about $8 plus labor).

The *broadening of constituencies* is one way of bringing people and designers, designers and needs, and end users and their products closer together.

Figure 1-13. (Facing page) *The instruction sheet by James Gilliland.* (Courtesy of Professor Hardcastle, Leeds Polytechnic, England)

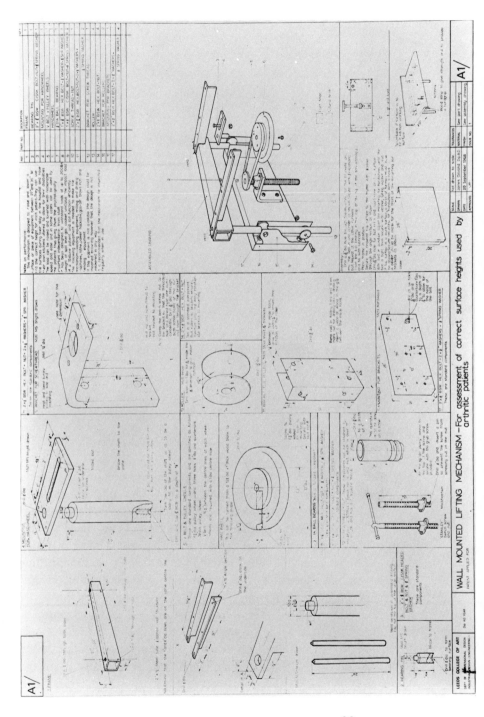

2
Design Participation

Whatever else He may have been, God was surely interdisciplinary.

ANON[1]

"PARTICIPATION" is a popular word now. Women, minority groups, and others who find themselves helplessly trapped in inhuman structures have started to demand participatory action. This need to be included in decision-making processes is fully justified and consumer demands have been met with varying amounts of understanding in areas such as medicine, law, urban planning, and architecture.

But industrial and graphic design are two fields that have responded slowly, if at all. The main reason for this is that consumers have failed to force these professionals to respond. And this lack of participation in the design process is due to the fact that most people do not know that designers exist and are equally unaware of the way in which design affects their lives.

The average consumer often has no clear concept of what design is all about. Not that people are foolish, but when a product appears in the marketplace, the fact that someone has actually designed and developed it is rarely mentioned. There are exceptions. In the Scandinavian countries, people tend to know that glassware, furniture, ceramics, and other products originate in the mind of a designer. In northern Europe, advertisements are frequently accompanied by the name of the designer. In Great Britain, Italy, and Germany, there is also a fairly high level of recognition of the people who originate the very best designs. But if the average Briton or Italian is confronted with something like a supermarket shopping cart, railroad carriage, filing cabinet, or surgical instrument, it is unlikely that he or she will think of its design origins.

Many people in the United States know even less about design. Although industry employs and values designers, the American public tends to associate design with home decoration, furnishings, and fashion. "Design?" they say. "Oh, you mean like wallpaper or repeat patterns on fabrics." The fact that so many people are ignorant about design complicates their participation in the design process. People cannot participate in something if they do not know it exists. One way of getting design and people closer together is to design things that make participation by end users essential to the design process. (The term "end user" is preferable to "consumer" because use connotes a less destructive meaning than consumption.)

In the long run, this means that designers and architects must be more accessible to people. It is the only way in which consumers can have a direct say in the design of products they will eventually use.

Design is a joyous, creative act. It concerns itself with problem solving and decision making. It provides the designer with enormous gratification to watch a concept move from the first explorative lines on a sheet of paper through different stages of development to an exacting, working prototype of the end product. But the problems facing designers are becoming increasingly complex, especially when the ecological, social, and political consequences are considered. I have said before that design is too important to be left to designers. But far from being a harsh judgment, this is a call for a higher standard of design. Because design must be both responsible and responsive, it must be performed by a team. But any team made up only of designers would be an ineffectual debating team. What is needed are nondesigners.

The idea is not new. For the past fifty years, industrial design and product development teams have involved sales managers, buyers, marketing executives, motivation research people, market analysts, production engineers, and comptrollers. The concept of a design team is nearly as old as the profession itself. Ideally, a design team should include people from all of the disciplines needed to solve the specific design problem. The team for designing a child's high chair, for instance, should include furniture makers, pediatricians, child psychologists, babies, and mothers in addition to a product designer well-versed in materials and processes.

The example of equipment designed by child psychologists to test children's locomotor responses may make the point. A square board has a seemingly random slit cut into it. A ½-inch wide slit meanders erratically all over the board. A child is given a ³⁄₁₆-inch wide stylus and asked to move it along the path from point A to point B within a given time and without touching the edges of the slit. Whenever the child touches the side of the slit, a shrill electric buzzer sounds. A response to failure has been designed into the testing apparatus. In 1980, I led a design team which, by consulting children directly, was able to redesign the test board (figure 2-1). Pathway, stylus, performance time, and task remained the same. The difference was that throughout the test, a tape played a pleasing tune. Whenever the child's stylus touched the edge, the music stopped. A pleasant reward had been substituted for a shrill and horrifying punishment. The children's test scores improved dramatically.

Consulting children directly is the operative phrase. A design team is not broad enough if it is merely interdisciplinary. It must also include some of the eventual end users.

Recently, the state of Missouri requested that sofas be designed and produced for housing shelters for the elderly and retirement homes. The purchasers were to be the owners and employees of these homes, and they insisted on unusually low seating units. Their reasons were quite openly stated: 'They're easier to take care of if they can't get out of their chairs'.[2] This bestial disregard

Figure 2-1. *My redesign of the testing rig for retarded children. Note the cassette tape player, which plays pleasant music as a reward instead of a shrill buzzer punishing failure. (Drawing by James Quiggins)*

of the needs of the end users is only possible when the end user is not a part of the design team.

The continuing process of democratizing design is not easy and is a slow process. The design, development, and construction of an exercising and play environment twelve years ago for spastic and paraplegic children in Finland clearly demonstrates the difficulties. The help of psychiatrists, therapists, psychologists, and nurses was not enough. A slow and tedious process of communicating directly with the handicapped children had to be developed. The different elements of the environment, including toys, were made and given to the children to play with. Their reactions were recorded verbally and photographically. Through continuous feedback from the children themselves, some colors were eliminated and others added. The children would say things like: "Sliding down that ramp is creepy!" Rather than responding, "Creepy in what way?" the ramp in question was tried out at different angles, different widths, and with different covering materials until it was evident that the children found the experience truly enchanting.

We discovered that some of the handicapped children could understand perspective drawings or simple sketches. Others needed three-dimensional scale models to understand. A few needed full-size mockups with the actual colors and coverings in order to form judgments. Once the communication bridge between the children and the design team was working, design and construction proceeded smoothly, with the resulting play environment proving highly successful.[3]

Even a design team that includes end users lacks one vital group—the workers who make the things the designer designs.[4] The democratization of the work place at Volvo in Sweden is one well known example. Another similar experiment was carried out recently by one of my clients, Bepla/Planet Products Pty. of Bellingen, New South Wales in Australia.

Brett Iggulden, the director and owner of the company that manufactures lamps, task lighting, and medical lamps, decided to enrich the work environment of his employees. Great difficulties with labor unions, worker apathy, and a general lack of motivation made him choose to move his small, seventy-employee factory from the gray concrete surroundings of industrial Melbourne to Bellingen, one of the loveliest country spots in New South Wales. Bellingen is only twenty miles from beaches, while a twenty-minute drive in the other direction brings you to the mountains. The town has roughly a thousand inhabitants, and has a near perfect climate.

The new factory building is situated on a lake, providing the workers with an enchanting view. The work force consists mostly of farmers' wives with a deep sense of motivation and young people who enjoy working in a place where swimming, mountain climbing, water skiing, and hiking literally begin at the factory gate.

Workers' suggestions are constantly sought by management. Changes in assembly procedures, design, or work schedules often originate from the factory floor. The management employs two designers and one design consultant (the management director is a trained designer himself) and shows a great willingness to innovate experiment. The ratio of designers to work force stands at 4:70, which is high and fairly rare. Management, together with the workers, try to keep to small production runs to avoid boredom. When a particular product becomes unexpectedly successful, larger production runs are subcontracted out to other manufacturers. This keeps the size of the work force and the number of items produced to a human scale.

Not only is the work force encouraged to initiate designs for lamps (see, for example, figure 2-2) and other products, but much of the handling machinery has also been designed and built by the workers. Because the workers are consulted at each stage of design development on ways of finding easier and better production methods, they not only believe that the products they are building are worthwhile, but that the company is as concerned with its work force as it is with its customers.

Designing for and with workers is far from simple. On a worldwide level, great differences exist between the relationship of management and their work force. In Sweden, for instance, workers are consulted about both their job and the environment in which they work. In such politically disparate countries as West Germany and The People's Republic of China, suggestions from the shop floor are not merely encouraged but actively sought. At Dartington Glass in North Devon, England, mixed teams of British and Swedish workers have for the past twenty years been forming themselves into small production teams of ten to twenty people and making suggestions to management about the working environment within the plant. Similar examples can be found in the United States, Japan, and Western and Eastern Europe.

Two examples, involving safety goggles and welding masks may demonstrate how workers can be consulted to help improve their comfort and work environment. Most protective eyeglasses and safety goggles are insensitively designed, giving the wearer the sinister look of Dr. Strangelove or Heinrich Himmler. They are usually uncomfortable, sweat producing, and ugly.

But compare them to ski goggles. Over 200 different models of ski goggles are available, including three that incorporate a tiny electronic fan or demister. Ski goggles are well designed in

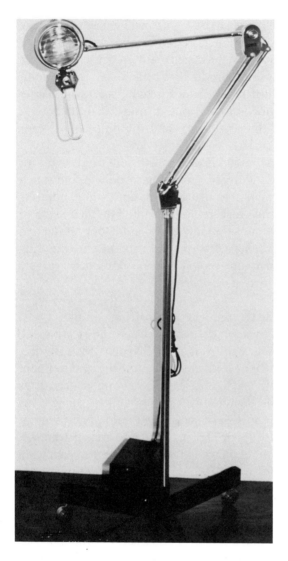

Figure 2-2. *Dental surgery or small operating-room lamp. Staff design, Planet Products, Bellingen, Australia. The light source is a standard motorcycle head-lamp, mounted on a flexible arm that also rotates a full 360°. The rolling base carries a standard twelve-volt car battery or a small transformer. This lamp sells well in Developing Countries in Asia, at a fraction of the price of its nearest competitor.*

terms of appearance, comfort, and durability. While the choice of ski goggles is large, workers in shops and factories are typically handed a pair of protective glasses with a design originating from 1934. The workers have a choice of wearing them and being uncomfortable or not wearing them and endangering their eyesight.

In 1974, an opinion poll was conducted in Great Britain among workers who needed eye protection. The participants were shown standard British and French safety glasses. A large majority requested that the glasses from France, well designed to be both safe and handsome, be made available to them. More importantly, they went on to wear them with pride. All workers are aware of the current trends in sunglass and eyeglass frames. It is hardly surprising that they reject present day safety glasses as cheap-looking and unattractive.[5]

Welding masks work in two ways—the dark vision panel protects the eyes and the large fiberboard or plastic shield keeps sparks or metal debris from reaching the welder's hair and face.

In 1973, one of my student groups talked to welders about the pros and cons of existing welding helmets. The majority felt that most masks were fiendishly uncomfortable and hot, although they felt that the protective function was adequate. As a result, most workers tended not to wear the masks except when they were actually using a torch or brazing gun. The meant that the workers' skin and hair were unprotected and their eyes were exposed to dangerously high light levels when not wearing their helmets as work was going on at adjacent welding stations.

One student, Roger Dalton, worked on assembly lines as a welder and observed other workers through long work days. From his hands-on experience and talks with union stewards, a new face protector was developed. The new design was nearly one third smaller and weighed only about half that of a traditional welding helmet (figure 2-3). By severely reducing the size and weight, the mask protected as much as the older version but was much more comfortable. The new shield moved up and down on a head track, making it easier to lift the mask out of the way. The head track was a lightweight aluminum product used in Royal Air Force flying helmets and was available as off-the-shelf hardware. The vision slot was darkened as in conventional welding

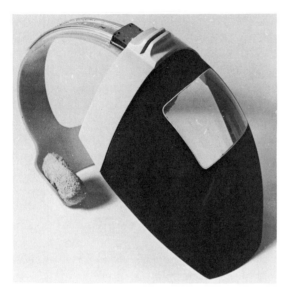

Figure 2-3. *The welding mask designed by Roger Dalton as a postgraduate student at Manchester Polytechnic.* (Photograph courtesy of Roger Dalton)

masks, but was enlarged slightly to provide greater peripheral vision.

In most factories safety products are introduced by management. This may be in response to new legislation, a safety inspection, or a serious accident. The desire for better working and better looking equipment must come directly from the workers, and be translated into better products through worker representation on design teams.

If a design team works sensitively and intelligently it can offer greater choice to end users. Their participation can be enlisted again by making it possible for them to do the actual product assembly. To house the poor, the federal government leveled slum neighborhoods and built vertical ghettos. In the early 1950s a series of high-rise buildings called Pruitt-Igoe were built in St. Louis. These crowded housing blocks were psychologically and physiologically damaging to their inhabitants. Mothers were afraid to let children play without supervision. The elevators became places of beatings and muggings for the elderly. The long, anonymous hallways disoriented people, increasing feelings of alienation and aggression. The area immediately surrounding the blocks was a combat zone where rape, narcotics trading, and juvenile delinquency were rife. Shopping centers were too far to reach on foot; few residents had cars and public transport was virtually nonexistent. Tenants were forced either to take expensive taxis or carry their groceries for miles. School, churches, and clinics were equally hard to reach.

After almost twenty years, the government finally agreed that the whole project was a fiasco. To the delight of the few unhappy residents and those architects who still felt people mattered, Missouri dynamited part of the development in 1972. But the sister blocks to Pruitt-Igoe, Wayne Miner, are still standing in Kansas City, Missouri. Wayne Miner consists of five of these concrete towers. Instead of blowing them up, the government has surrounded them with hundreds of low one- and two-story townhouses, gently landscaped and surrounded by lawn and trees, making the arrangement at least bearable.

When the residents of Wayne Miner asked me to design some decent, low cost furniture, I asked some students to actually move into the apartments in the high-rise development. By developing a dialogue with the residents while designing and building the chairs, a series of priorities evolved. It was decided to develop an easy chair made from half a sheet of plywood (four-foot square) and two yards of linen canvas (figure 2-4). Each chair was to be accompanied by a visual instruction sheet that would show how to build the chair. These chairs were then built by the residents.

A simple desk or study lamp, casting a direct light beam and using a low watt bulb, was also designed (figure 2-5). A student developed a flat pattern that could be sprung into a three dimensional shade and base combination. Made of plastic or plasticized paper, the lamp can be made in ten minutes. When the bulb has been screwed into the socket and the cord plug and lines have been attached, the result is a handsome, functional lamp for less than $3.

We left Wayne Miner believing that we had completed a satisfactory job, and were therefore surprised when we revisited the development five years later to learn that the lamp was still being used everywhere, but almost none of the chairs were left. We asked the residents if the chairs had broken or had been uncomfortable, and they told us that the chairs had been quite comfortable

39

Figure 2-4. *First chair developed for residents of Wayne Miner housing development. Designed by Jim Murray as a student at the Kansas City Art Institute.*

Figure 2-5. *Do-it-yourself study lamp. Designed by Melissa Duffner as a student at the Kansas City Art Institute.*

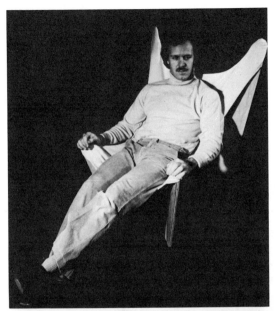

Figure 2-6. *A successful attempt to provide seating of the "Safari,"* Hardoy, *or "Butterfly" type for Wayne Miner residents. The chair has been simplified greatly, is easy to build, and very comfortable. Designed by Randall Cohen as a student at the Kansas City Art Institute.*

Figure 2-7. *The three parts of Randall Cohen's chair.*

Figure 2-8. *Assembly instructions for Randall Cohen's chair.*

Figure 2-9. *The "family chair." As described, "Father builds the wooden structure, Mother sews the canvas sausages and the children stuff the sausages with old stockings or clean rags. The whole family then assembles the chair." Designed at the Kansas City Art Institute.*

Figure 2-10. *Assembly instructions for the "family chair."*

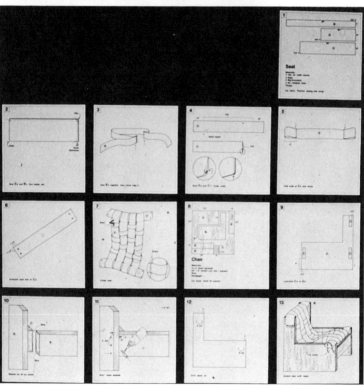

and had worn well, but that they did not like them. What the design students had considered beautiful, the end users had found ugly. The residents felt that the chairs looked like third rate do-it-yourself furniture, not like what they thought "normal" chairs should look like.

The world of the poor and the elderly is a strange one to most design students. In this case, the students had failed to take into account the users' ideas of beauty. So, four years later, new chairs were designed. This time the residents were consulted more thoroughly, resulting in chair designs that were comfortable, inexpensive, attractive, and easy to build (figures 2-6–10). The users did not think they looked handmade or unfinished. The designers had learned to deal with real people in a real situation. Participation worked both ways.

Participation in design is based on trust. Although most people are inexperienced in design and are not used to working with designers, the design profession must reach out and ease the way for dialogue. The task is difficult, but it is absolutely essential if design is not to bankrupt itself morally. Only in this way will the designer become a tool in the hands of the people.

3
Curing Product Addiction

How much does a person lack himself who feels the need to have so many things.

RIKYU

THERE are too many products. Too much energy, too many irreplaceable resources, and too much creative talent is involved in making them. Enormous pollution results during the production cycle and when we throw the products away, when their useful life has ended. Yet product addiction is comparatively new, a development of the postwar years. Product junkies are as numerous in West Germany, Holland, Canada, Australia, and Japan as in America. In Great Britain, even in the middle of a severe recession, people are still hooked on buying and filling their homes with useless gadgets.

Department stores, specialty shops and suburban discount centers are glutted with a mind-blinding array of useless gimmicky products. Looking at the increasingly frantic attempts of manufacturers to unload useless junk on consumers, one wonders when and how it will all stop. Some of our homes are so overstuffed with electronic and mechanical trivia that we conduct garage sales every spring just to get rid of the accumulated garbage. From automatic coffeemakers, battery-powered flour sifters, and electric spoons to Star Wars-inspired electronic scanners, the list is endless.

For an industrial designer, the temptation is strong to cry, "enough!" With inflation, pollution, and energy costs, why not stop the flow of new products altogether? The designer could simply withdraw his talents from the marketplace entirely. Or he could continue to design blindly, without any thought of the consequences. Because people have been trained, wooed, cajoled, threatened, irritated, and subliminally manipulated into becoming product addicts, it makes sense to many designers to use their training to satisfy the spurious needs generated by a hard-core, hard-sell advertising industry.

A third alternative for the designer is to decide what he wants to design and why. Since many of these choices are situational and existential, this is far from easy. There are no guidelines, no simple answers. Nor is it an easy choice among these three alternatives. Many young designers are driven by financial need to grind out superfluous junk. Others, not as harried economically, choose the first option and stop designing altogether. Choosing the third alternative—designing things that make sense—is the most difficult decision of all. It is a new direction, with no signposts and few precedents. Obviously, few designers choose this socially rewarding but financially precarious option.

Design philosophy and the designer's self-image have changed dramatically. Some twenty years ago, designers saw themselves primarily as artists, able to close the gap between technology and marketing through their concern with form, function, color, texture, harmony, and proportion. For industrial designers and architects, there were also the considerations of cost, convenience, and current tastes. Within ten years, the designer's role had broadened into a system approach, showing greater interest in production, distribution, market research, and sales. This opened the door to team design, even if the team was largely made up of technocrats; sales specialists and modish persuaders.

In the western world, the idea that there is a difference between designing and making things is only about 250 years old. During that time, design has been increasingly connected to the appreciation of things deemed "beautiful" by those segments of society given to establishing moral and ethical bases for the concept of beauty. Louis Sullivan's "form follows function," Frank Lloyd Wright's "form and function are one" and "truth to material," and the Bauhaus dictum "fitness for purpose" and "unity in diversity" were all basically ethical and moral imperatives. Often the moral imperatives ousted the practical reality, as anyone who has ever sat on a Frank Lloyd Wright chair or tried to read by a Bauhaus Kugellicht can testify.

Millions of people have substituted the satisfaction of owning things or spending money for any meaningful reward in life. Most things are not designed for the needs of people, but for the needs of manufacturers to sell to people. This important shift of emphasis has occurred during the last three decades. "They want production to be limited to 'useful things,' but forget that the production of too many 'useful' things results in too many 'useless' people." Karl Marx's observation still rings true. With the belief that one gadget will solve all of our difficulties, we have destroyed our capacity to strive for new solutions.

Returning to the United States after several years in Europe, I was immediately struck by advertisements and catalogs extolling the virtues of their merchandise with descriptions such as: "for that real leather look," or "for the fine feel of suede," or "the look of real silk with the convenience of . . ."(some sort of polyester?). Nothing was real, nothing had quality—it was all fake.

When it comes to products, ugliness is often more than skin deep. A major change is taking place. Quality, safety, performance, utility, and product life all seem to have been lost in the reshuffle. A product sells if:

1. It's *brand new* and does things *fast*.

2. It makes life (work, job, whatever) *easier* and more *convenient*.

3. It *looks great* (whatever that means).

This attitude has spawned scores of 'new' concepts—hot dog cookers (figure 3-1), electronic fish scalers (figure 3-2), donut fryers, hydraulic log-splitters (figure 3-3), carving knives with headlights, electric carrot peelers (which must be worked more slowly than the manual kind, and are harder to clean), electronic shoe horns and battery-driven toilet rolls that dispense tissues with horoscopes printed on them.

Without doubt, some scientist is hard at work right now developing the ultimate electronic grapefuit knife, a vibrator to massage the backs of people driving to the supermarket, an electric page turner for comic books, or a forty-eight-inch television set that looks like a Mongolian officer's desk at the time of Tamburlaine. Many products today are shoddily made, rarely perform their

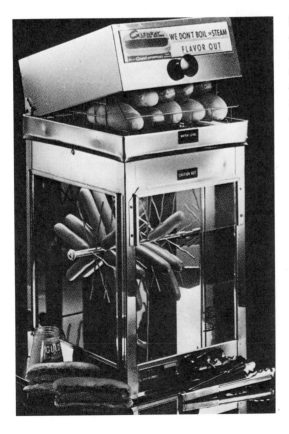

Figure 3-1. *A wonderful electric machine that will rotate and grill fifty-six hotdogs simultaneously and costs less than $300 (designed and manufactured in the United States).*

Figure 3-2. *A wall-mounted electronic fish scaler for the busy housewife (designed and manufactured in the United States).*

Figure 3-3. *For almost $300, outdoor types can buy this "hydraulic log-splitter" to cut their firewood (designed and manufactured in the United States).*

ridiculously limited jobs, and usually break down or are discarded before their warranties expire.

When *all-brand-new-latest*, *fast-easy-convenient*, or *great looks* are not the sales pitches, then the products are usually designed to look like known quality objects.

One of the more cynical advertisements perpetrated by the US automobile industry was a two-page, full-color spread in *Time* in 1977.[1] Under the headline, "Which is the impressive new $20,000 Mercedes Benz?" and "Can you tell the Ford Granada ESS from a $20,000 Mercedes Benz?," twelve small pictures were arranged in quiz form. Each pair of pictures made a visual comparison. These picture-pair comparisons were supposed to establish that Detroit's fake Mercedes looked like the original, but it was all surface styling.

Design decisions by Mercedes-Benz were taken to make their car function well and to provide the driver with safety, comfort and aesthetic satisfaction. What the advertisement failed to show was that the design decisions on the Ford Granada were only made superficially to make their car look like a Mercedes-Benz. What the advertisement really said was: "Mercedes-Benz has developed and designed a beautiful, safe, and well-engineered car. We at Ford can sell you a cheaper copy of it that almost looks like the original."

A lot has changed in the auto industry since that advertisement appeared six years ago. With nearly half a million Americans in the automobile industry (or automobile-related fields) laid off, temporarily furloughed, or just plain unemployed, Detroit tells us that if only we would stop buying those Japanese and European imports, then thousands of workers would get back to work, our balance-of-payments deficits would reverse, and automobile executives would again enjoy three-martini lunches and our whole economy might surge forward.

Great. But just try to find a purebred American car these days. Detroit's glib hype, as usual, hides their advocating a double standard. We are supposed to stay away from foreign cars while they, the carmakers, are busily shopping around for foreign car parts to build into their so-called American cars: Chrysler's *Horizon* and *Omni* subcompacts use German engines, starters, and transmissions, *Aries* and *Reliant* use engines from Japan. General Motors *Chevettes* use French transmissions, and Japanese diesel engines will power future versions. Recently, GM went to the expense of building a new factory in Singapore (what about American workers now?) to make radio parts.

Ford had a better idea: Their new *Escort* uses British steering parts, Spanish front suspension components, Italian Fuel pumps, front-drive systems, and steering wheels from Japan. The radios are Korean. What does that leave? A glove compartment, wheels, tires, and a body that closely resemble German/Italian styling! And of course the upholstery and the foam-rubber dice that dangle from the mirror. And American Motors is collaborating with Renault on a car, the Alliance, that will draw half of its parts from France.

But let's get back to Ford. A secret internal memo that leaked out dealt with their study of possible sources for four-cylinder engines. Their four choices boiled down to: buying a Japanese-designed engine from Japan; building the Japanese engine in Mexico; building a French engine in Mexico; or, as a final reluctant choice, building the Japanese engine in America.

The big four save billions of dollars a year by buying foreign car parts keeping American workers out of jobs and throwing the economy into chaos. They preach "buy American" but practice buying abroad.

So don't ask me to invest in an American car. I've already got about $45 of my family's tax money invested in bailing out the Chrysler Corporation.

This erosion of workmanship and quality, together with a systematic flooding of the consumer market with trivial merchandise, has created two new problems. Americans (when given a choice) are seeking quality abroad and foreigners are buying fewer American goods. When the deutsche mark was high and the dollar low in 1980, German consumers began buying American-made cars. Within a few months this buying spree ended, and a German consumer was quoted in *Time*: "They are poorly finished, parts don't fit well, and there are permanent rattles that my dealer says he can't get rid of." The Japanese now demand that American-made cars have an extra twelve coats of paint and lacquer applied before they buy them.[2]

Let's look at the product choices made by an average upper-middle-income family in Arizona.

Rick Chambers (not his real name) sells insurance and owns his own insurance brokerage firm. His wife teaches retarded children. Both are in their mid-forties, have three children and lead a comfortable upper-middle-class life. A survey of the products they have purchased over the years shows what people will buy when they have enough money to choose what they want. Note the countries of origin.

Rick is an amateur photographer. He owns two German cameras and a Swedish Hassleblad. The camera lenses are German and Swedish. His slide projector is made by Leitz, a West German firm. Their stereo system is made by Bang & Olufsen of Copenhagen, their cassette tape unit by Sonab of Sweden. The typewriters and adding machine in Rick's office are made by Olivetti of Italy. At home he has an Olivetti portable made in Spain under Italian franchise. His pocket calculator is made by Sinclair of Great Britain. His ballpoint pen, fountain pen, and pencil set are by Lamy of West Germany.

His eyeglasses have Dutch frames; his wife's frames are Swedish. The Chambers own two automobiles—a Mercedes-Benz and a Honda CVCC. Both of their watches are Swiss. Mrs. Chambers' sewing machine is by Yamaha, the same Japanese firm that made their piano and their oldest son's Moog-type synthesizer. Her hair dryer was made in Italy; the bathroom scale in the Irish Republic. There are three bicycles in the family—two are English, one is French.

In the kitchen, Mrs. Chambers uses an imported Cuisinart electric food processor and a German coffee maker by Braun (the same firm that makes their coffee grinder and her husband's electric razor). Their nonmechanical kitchen tools—wooden spoons, wire whisks, and stirrers—come from Yugoslavia, Portugal, Spain, France, Austria, and Poland. Their clay stewing pots come from Greece; the pans from France, Finland, and Germany. The kitchen scale is French, as are the chef's knives. Their British dishes stand in a Swedish dish rack along with the Danish flatware and the Finnish glasses (which are washed in a Miele electric dishwasher from Germany). The kitchen also contains an orange juice squeezer from Sweden and shears by Fiskars of Finland.

Most of the Chambers' furniture comes from Denmark, Sweden, and Finland. Rick's office chairs are German and move on castors made by Kevi of Finland.

It would take too long to list all of their clothing, but most of their luggage, purses and pocketbooks are made in France, Italy, and Spain. Rick's cotton shirts come from England and Switzerland and his leather jackets from Spain and Israel. Mrs. Chambers' winter coat comes from Iceland and the children's bulky sweaters from Ireland. Nearly all of these foreign goods were purchased in the States. The Chambers have not traveled abroad extensively since their three-week honeymoon in France and England fourteen years ago.

Domestic needs apart, there are whole professions whose routine tools come from abroad. In design and architecture, for instance, nearly all technical precision pens (Rotring, Rapidograph, Staedtler, Polygraph, Mars,) are made in Germany. Drafting instruments usually come from Switzerland, Germany, Britain, or Japan. Many paint brushes and pigments come from Holland, France, Italy, and England.

In sports, cross country skis come from Norway and Finland. Some of the best gliders are made in Germany, Finland and Rumania. Shotguns come from Britain, Spain, and Italy; ski boots from Italy; hockey helmets, face masks, and other protective gear from Canada.

Goods made in this country in many cases tend to sell to the bottom end of the market. All over the country people with glazed eyes are pushing shopping carts and listening to Mantovani while strolling down the aisles of discount stores, looking to buy *anything* as long as it's cheap. Going to church has been replaced by going to the store, as a social event. One reason is that a large part of the population finds self-fulfillment in buying. The shop has been turned into an arena of sounds, light shows, and pro-motional theatre.

The present economic depression has changed these habits somewhat. People in general now shop for specific items at discount stores and remnant shops. This change in shopping patterns has brought home one sobering fact to people living in smaller cities in the Midwest and South: Frequently if there is nothing to shop for, there is literally nothing else to do on a weekend. This may be a partial explanation for the success of Pac Man and other electronic coin guzzlers and ever-growing numbers of cultural delinquents.

Americans abroad are often stunned by the United States influence they find everywhere—Louis Armstrong's horn wailing in countless boutiques from Amsterdam to Bandung; Levis from London to Leningrad; milk shakes in Shanghai and Cairo. The "Cocacolonization" of the planet is in full swing.

It is no longer a novelty to find a Colonel Sanders, fried-chicken franchise restaurant on the winding shopping streets of Japan or Indonesia, and the streets of Auckland, New Zealand are now enriched by the presence of Pizza Huts. The visually unobtrusive streetscapes of Cologne, Milan, and Zagreb suffer from garish presence of Taco Bells and Burger Chefs. Recently I witnessed the opening of McDonald's first restaurant in the sleepy town of Goraka in Papua New Guinea. American folk rock, hard rock, acid rock and rockabilly blare out from shopfronts in London, Düsseldorf, Copenhagen, and Warsaw. American horror comics sell briskly in European and Asian countries where they have not yet been outlawed as sadistic and violent. Dallas, Love Boat, Flamingo Road, Fantasy Island, and Kojak assault bewildered audiences in Sri Lanka, Nigeria, and Lebanon.

Airports in Europe and Southeast Asia bristle with 747s, 707s, and other American airplanes. At the far end of the same airports you can watch American tanks, armored personnel carriers, fighter planes, computers, and other military hardware being unloaded.

Although Lincolns, Cadillacs, and Buicks are still flown to the oil-rich Middle East, it is rare to come across an American car in western or northern Europe. In Finland, Denmark, Austria, and Portugal, the sight of such an automobile usually indicates the arrival of the United States Ambassador, the presence of our troops or the visit of an American film star. On the whole, Europeans and Asians do not buy our cars.

We dominate the market of airplanes, military hardware, films, records, earth moving equipment, computers, and franchised fast-food chains in western Europe and Japan. But what about American furniture, dishes, pots and pans, radios, stereo equipment, television sets, clothing, toys, stoves, vacuum cleaners, refrigerators, automobiles, and other everyday objects. Are there no American-made domestic products that overseas customers will buy?

In the United States, quality-conscious consumers are beginning to shop in stores that specialize in imported kitchen and dining equipment. Japanese and Italian goods are quite popular in this country. All this merchandising is part of the growing consumer rebellion against shoddy American merchandise.

Of course, the ironic thing is that "made in USA" was once so powerful a guarantee of quality that, according to technological folklore, in the 1930s the Japanese built a town called USA so that they could put the magic imprint on their merchandise. Model A and Model T Fords were splendidly engineered, well-designed, and nearly fail-safe. These cars were inexpensive and easy to maintain and repair. The DC-3 airplane was the Model A of the airways—so safe and easy to operate that in 1981, twenty years after it was phased out, China began building copies for developing countries.

New versions of the Franklin stove, developed in the American colonies around 1760, are now being made here and in Denmark, Norway, Great Britain, and Canada. Canadian and Alaskan Eskimos still use hundred-year-old Winchester carbines as their preferred hunting weapon. Both the Kodak Box Brownie camera and the Gillette safety razor set world standards for nearly seventy years. The classic folding director's chair (still made by the Telescope Furniture Company and by Gold Medal some seventy-five years later), spawned adaptations in Finland, Germany, Denmark, and Sweden. The unconditionally guaranteed Zippo lighter, the contemporary furniture produced by Herman Miller and Knoll International, Peter Schlumbohm's Chemex coffeemaker, the United States Army's 1941 jeep vehicle, and the first Polaroid camera can all be added to this list of successful American products.

It is extremely difficult to find contemporary American consumer products that show the same design innovation as these examples from the last 230 years. The Japanese, once known for their cheap imitations of American and European products, have abandoned the town of USA. They are now bringing a tremendous amount of inventiveness and ingenuity to their own cameras, TV sets, microscopes, classical guitars, stereo systems, cars, trucks, and farm machinery. Many of these products are creatively conceived and of high quality.

This is best shown by an example from the field of professional camera design. In the early 1950s, photographers interested in buying an expensive Hassleblad (a precision $2\frac{1}{4}'' \times 2\frac{1}{4}''$ camera made in Sweden) eagerly awaited a Japanese copy called Bronica. When the Bronica arrived on the market, it was surprisingly priced nearly at the same level as the Hassleblad. The Swedish company then sued Nippon Kigatu—only to find that the court decided that the Japanese Bronica included more than 180 new ideas and innovations that were protected by patents. Hassleblad lost its case. There are other examples that show that the Japanese are no longer just "good copiers and not innovators." In the automotive field most Japanese cars *exceed* U.S. government standards for emission control, warning lights, and seat belts even though American car manufacturers still routinely testify that these same standards are unrealistic and unreachable.

Volumes have been written on the differences between European and American worker morale as opposed to the spirit that motivates their Japanese counterparts. Scores of articles and pamphlets have investigated the internal working organization of Japanese factories, the amount of government encouragement and intervention in Japanese manufactured goods, and the relative wages paid to workers.

What is important is the amount of risk Japanese management is willing to take, and this is reflected in the work of their designers. Portable radios designed in Western Europe and North America seem to come in two versions, with too few control knobs or with too many. In the United States, radios are sold in three cosmetically different versions. One of these might be fairly plain and this model might be marketed as "modern." Another version made from plastic veneers with the look of "antique walnut" might have the speaker grill covered with a brass or copper screen and would be marketed as "early American" or "French provincial." A third version (and please remember that we are talking about radios that are absolutely identical, except for surface styling) with brushed aluminum knobs, a black foam speaker grill and sleek lines would sell as "high tech."

By contrast, the Japanese have worked out how, when, where, and why radios are used. This has given us bright yellow twistable bracelet-radios, AM/FM sets contained in headphones (perfect for joggers), and radios that have floppy beanbag bottoms (ideal for placing in the transmission well of a sports car). There are clock radios, radio cassette combinations that tape directly from the radio, radio cassette combinations that can copy (dub) a second tape simultaneously, AM/FM radios that fit easily into a waistcoat pocket—the list is endless. Admittedly, some of these ideas are just silly, and some have only highly specialized applications. But instead of trying to design one radio that will suit many Europeans and Americans, Japanese designers have developed scores of different versions. Each acts as a trial balloon, and many have found a permanent niche. Without exception, quality control on all these radios is very high.

By contrast, the quality of most European and American radios may not be as high. And unfortunately, this isn't only true of radios. One of the reasons we do not get quality is that we no longer expect it. We used to buy cars to last three or four years, a refrigerator to last twenty years and a toaster until it wears out. Compare this with the Electrolux refrigerator made in Sweden and unavailable in the United States. It has no moving parts, no fan, no compressor. You plug it in and it does its job noiselessly. A friend in Ireland has used his since 1937. In forty-four years it has never needed a repair.

Sometimes price becomes more important than quality. In 1975 a new wrist watch called Porsche was introduced for men and women. It consisted of a black instrumentlike face enclosed in a mat black anodized aluminum case. The watch connoted high precision, excellent craftsmanship, durability, and quality. It was designed and made in West Germany and now sells for $275. Within months of its appearance, a copy from Taiwan, marketed under the illegal misleading name Porshe was introduced. It flooded American and European markets and now sells for $19.95. In the United States the $275 watch has virtually been driven from the market. In Western Europe, the Taiwanese watch has not sold because it only looks like the real thing, but is badly made and does not work well.

Frequently, a quality product and its counterfeit look-alike are sold side by side. This turns the whole quality game into an argument between informed quality awareness on one hand, and status aspirations on the other. In Mexico and many South American countries, painstaking copies of Cartier watches, Yves St. Laurent scarves, and Gucci loafers and handbags are manufactured and sold. In Ecuador, iron-on designer labels can be bought at most shops to turn a $9 pair of blue jeans into Jordache "originals." Phony Izod-LaCoste alligators have been sold in Italy for around fifty cents a dozen.

Originally, makers' labels were simple marks of identification. Later, these identifying marks became associated with certain standards of quality. It is only during the last thirty-five years or so that a further regrettable change has taken place. Labels that insure quality have become status symbols in themselves. Because of this it is easy to see how trademarks have become the crucial part of the product or garment to be counterfeited. But the root cause of the disappearance of quality lies deeper. Much of western society (from the chairman of the board down to the lowliest paid helper on the assembly line) has now substituted the satisfaction that money can buy for other, deeper satisfactions.

One of the greatest satisfactions in life is a job well done, a task accomplished superbly. Watch a one-year old learning how to walk; a potter finishing a vase; a surgeon performing a complex operation; a sailplane pilot searching for and finding a strong thermal updraught; an archer hitting the bullseye; a sportsman landing his golden speckled trout; a cook creating a perfect souffle; a craftsman completing a fine piece of furniture. This is fulfillment, derived from a certain ecstasy in that moment.

Personal pride in craftsmanship and high quality goods on the part of workers is difficult to maintain—the weekly paycheck and what it will buy are more important. Does the modern mechanic feel remorse when he sits down to supper because he is unsure about the repairs he did on an automobile that day? Does the director of a large corporation worry about the fact that their instant coffeemaker is not really needed, is shoddily made, and consumes 18% more energy than the earlier unit? Or is he or she concerned about the bottom line or about a new country home or an around-the-world tour? Do shoppers fastidiously examine competing brands, read *Which?* or *Consumer Reports*, study instruction manuals, and make mature purchasing decisions? Or do they shuffle around the local discount store, mesmerized by advertising and lulled by Muzak background music, looking for the biggest, shiniest, cheapest thing to purchase?

Most of the new generation of electric kitchen gadgets illustrate the point. No one *needs* an electric taco steamer. But some company may develop, build, and produce it. Heavy magazine advertising and television ad blitzes will promote it, and a few million sales later, when the last of these gourmets' delights has stopped functioning, the manufacturer will pull out of the market, giggling all the way to the bank. If the gimmick is unusually successful, he may launch Mark II—with warning lights, an enchilada warming drawer, and a unit that plays The Mexican Hat Dance when the burritos are ready.

This mass advertising and merchandising of trivia is filling the marketplace and the shopper's mind. Many of these gadgets are made by "quick dip" manufacturers, that is, companies that are set up to mass produce some shoddy gift item, saturate the market as fast as possible, and then get out quickly. In the world of consumer products, the bad often drives out the good, meaning that people looking for quality frequently have little choice. This changes attitudes towards buying, owning, maintaining, repairing, and finally throwing things away.

Among technologically developed countries, quality awareness seems to be lowest in the Soviet Union, the United States, Israel, Australia, South Africa, and Canada. Although these countries have unique national and racial roots, dissimilar political systems and population differences that are truly staggering, they have one thing in common—these countries are pioneering societies. Historically, they have shared the pragmatic approach of people facing the frontier. This pioneer approach asks the primary question: does it work? Fitness for purpose is the only standard in a pioneering society, whether it is also an elegant solution is unimportant. The tool, once it has served its purpose, will be tossed away. While fitness for purpose is one way of judging the excellence of a product, if it is the only evaluative criterion, refinement never takes place.

World War II and subsequent wars gave rise to the concept

of plug-in, plug-out components in military hardware. A disabled bomber airplane, limping back to its airbase during the war, could not be kept on the ground long for lengthy repairs. Instead, damaged parts would be removed and replaced with new parts. While this method of repairing things saved time, it was enormously wasteful, because the damaged components were usually scrapped. This mentality of wastefulness (so necessary in war) has drifted into peacetime product design, and the approach has found favor in the pioneering countries mentioned above. The British will usually try to repair things, and fixing broken parts is an absolute necessity in developing countries. In the United States, many components in household appliances and automobiles have been specifically designed to be unfixable and to be scrapped when they fail.

One factor that contributes to high quality is meticulous quality control at the factory. This means the rejection of faulty units, and to cut down on the number of faulty units requires worker participation and a high level of interest and motivation. This in turn influences the initial design thinking.

Compare two automatic coffeemakers, one made in West Germany and the other in the United States. There are major differences in appearance and performance, these differences having been designed in at the start. The West German firm is small, their workers sit on the company board, and are deeply interested in what the product looks like and how it sells at home and abroad. (Part of Braun's merchandizing operation in the United States is now owned by Gillette; however since the Gillette company is requiring Braun to drop its name from some of the products sold here, this Braun–Gillette marriage is surely headed for the divorce courts. *All* the design is still done by Dieter Rams in Frankfurt.) The machine (figure 3-4) is precision matched for careful assembly, so that separation lines (the lines where two parts of the case come together) barely show.

The American unit (figure 3-5) is designed to have broad separation lines between the various parts, and these are heavily indented so that the bad joins of misaligned parts are recessed into dark, shadowy areas. This makes "bash and fit" assembly possible, allowing for tolerance errors of as much as an eighth

Figure 3-4. *Coffee maker made by Braun of West Germany. Note the clean and minimal lines.* (*Photograph by John Charlton*)

of an inch. As a result, the product rejection rate is kept comfortably low. This coffeemaker is made more "attractive" with cheap, flashy chromium strips and extra buttons.

A second example involves food processors. One of the best units is made in France and sells for $200 (figure 3-6). A domestic model (figure 3-7) costs ninety dollars (both prices as of October 1981). On a simple economic level, the difference seems to be in favor of the American unit, but the French machine carries a guarantee period of thirty years when the customer can return the unit for repair at the company's expense. The American unit carries a limited warranty of three months. Parts and labor are additional, and the unit has to be insured and shipped back to the maker at the owner's expense. But that's not all. The French food processor has no switches—it is started and stopped by engaging the mixing bowl. Another American counterpart (figure 3-8) has fourteen switches relayed through a master switch, making twenty-eight different, and fairly useless, settings possible.

It is often said that imported products outsell American ones partly because of the lower wages paid abroad. In fact, this is

Figure 3-5. *"Mr. Coffee" coffee maker. Note the overhangs and deep recesses, designed to hide sloppy separation lines. This indicates "bash-and-fit" assembly. Also note digital control timer and six-way switches (designed in the United States, manufactured in South Korea, Taiwan and Hong Kong.)*
(Photograph by John Charlton)

often a red herring. Wages in Sweden, Denmark, Finland, and West Germany are frequently higher than those paid in the United States. Japanese industrial salaries are rising fast and are now (according to a recent issue of *Time* devoted entirely to Japanese industrial practice) surpassing those in the United States.

In general, a good deal of the small, frugal product design still comes from Finland, the Scandinavian countries, Germany, Italy, Japan, and Great Britain. Typically, some design schools in the United States consider designing flatware, an ashtray, a small nonelectrical and nonmechanical toy, or a better clothes hanger, entirely beneath their notice. Simple domestic articles like alarm clocks, chef's knives, portable radios, or thermometers (on which European and Asian schools spend so much time) fall into the same category. Understandably, designing large systems pays better than perfecting the ultimate chef's knife, unless the joy of coming to grips with design on a level that will affect people most directly outweighs the desire for cash. It is reassuring that this element of joy found in perfecting simple objects is becoming more important to young designers and students.

Figure 3-6. *Cuisinarts' CFP-5 food processor. Note the complete absence of any switches.* (Photograph courtesy of Cuisinarts, Inc., Greenwich, Connecticut)

Figure 3-7. *General Electric food processor. Note nine different switches.* (Photograph by John Charlton)

Figure 3-8. *Like something from the Starship Enterprise: the "master control panel" of an American food processor/blender with fifteen switches that make twenty-eight combinations possible.* (Photograph by John Charlton)

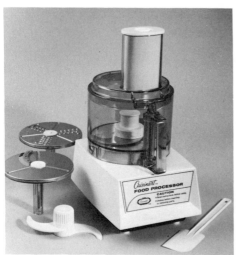

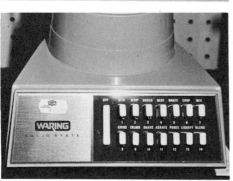

It is this element of joy that is helping turn things around. New forces are making themselves felt in bringing about higher quality products and more quality awareness among consumers. The first indications are coming from artists, craftsmen, the young, and those obsessively dedicated to ideals. Although an enormous amount of money is lost due to imports, there are still few signs of industry realizing that, in a depression economy, quality is becoming more important to people (always assuming that such decent quality does not increase price beyond all reason).

In the United States we are experiencing a renaissance of quality. We have wrongfully written off expectations of quality in many domestic products, but the cheap, low quality merchandise we buy instead has freed some disposable income, which we are increasingly investing in crafts. From hand-thrown ceramic containers, ashtrays, and wine goblets to woven hangings, placemats, bed covers, and hand-carved coffee tables, we are witnessing a major resurgence of crafts.

Craft objects fill an interesting niche in design. Craftsmen explore new directions and new materials frequently stretching traditional materials to their limits. Not all of these products are good. Some are sloppy and some are complete failures, but as a visit to any exhibition of handcrafted objects will show, a craftsman feels responsible for the object he or she creates.

In *Future Shock* Alvin Toffler pointed out that we are moving from a product centered to a post-industrial society where our concerns center around services and experiences.[3] In the renaissance of quality awareness, there is evidence that he was right.

Shops that deal with special experience-connected needs are springing up all over the United States and Great Britain. Walk into a place that specializes in backpacking or rock-climbing equipment and you will often be greeted by young, knowledgeable, and enthusiastic salespeople who are eager to advise you on the merits or faults of each piece of equipment. Bicycle shops in university towns like Madison, Wisconsin, Cambridge, Massachusetts, or Berkeley, California, have become community centers with information on safety, local rallies, and new equipment, and serve as meeting places for community political action groups campaigning for bicycle paths and safety legislation. Gourmet food shops and stores dealing with organically grown health foods are ready to assist customers with recipes, diet plans, and cooking tips. Old style florist shops (ready to sell a funeral wreath or a gardenia for Saturday night's prom) are giving way to 'botanical clinics' willing to take in your failing *monstera deliciosa* and gently nurse it back to health. Stereo shops, stores specializing in model making, hang gliding, spelunking, and other leisure activities have become more like clubs than retail shops. This indicates a revolution in both merchandising methods and lifestyles, with a high emphasis on knowledge, service, experience and, most of all, quality. So maybe the response to the question "where has all the quality gone?" is not one simple answer, but has many answers:

1. Some people have moved into the do-it-yourself market. An executive in the oil industry is proud of the grandfather clock that stands in the hallway of his home. It is the second clock he has built, having made the first one from a kit "in order to understand how it works." He built his second clock from scratch and inlaid it with various tropical hardwoods. He explains that he built it himself because he could do a better job than an assembly line clockmaker, he could do it less expensively, and the result would be more personal and look more the way he wanted it to. He adds, "If something goes wrong, I know what to do to fix it because I've built it myself."

2. Some quality (as explained previously with examples from Europe and Japan) has moved abroad.

3. Some quality has moved to the crafts.

The apocalyptic horrors of inflation, depression, dwindling resources, and high energy costs can be viewed as challenges and opportunities to wean product junkies away from their preoccupation with materialism.

In the mid-1960s, it was my task to work with a cross-disciplinary team to try to work out what sort of large kitchen appliances Americans would buy during the 1980s. This was done at the request of one of the largest retail merchandising organizations in the United States. It is always hazardous to predict the future, but certain strong trends seemed evident. Among the social and demographic tendencies we noted were the women's liberation movement (meaning a greater number of working wives and mothers), the increase of convenience food and quick service restaurants, the shortage of raw materials due to the rising cost of energy, and the near disappearance of decent repair facilities for broken appliances.

As a result of our findings, we told our client that during the 1980s and 1990s most large appliances would probably be purchased by contractors, developers, and landlords rather than by individuals or families. We were convinced that during the time period indicated, people in the United States and Canada (the market for which the report was prepared), would expect to find large appliances such as stoves, refrigerators, freezers, dishwashers, and washing machines in the apartments, condominiums, and houses in which they lived.

By anticipating how the purchasing criteria would change (assuming that condominium managers and apartment house owners would make up the bulk of the purchasing public), we were able to develop simple product guidelines:

1. Appliances had to be built to last, without annual or triannual model changes. Artificial obsolescence was on the way out.

2. Appliances had to be energy efficient.

3. Appliances had to be sturdily built and easy to maintain.

4. Repairs had to be simple, so that a minimum repair and maintenance staff would be required.

5. Aesthetically, the units had to be unobtrusive and simple. In many cases, they would be permanently built in, thus reducing the amount of materials and resources needed for "shroud" design (the sides, top and back that enclose the unit).

All of the criteria developed for this large, profit-oriented corporation are criteria that demand a more ecologically responsible technology. In addition, these appliances, though no longer owned by individuals, can help cure product addiction.

Since these reports and studies were submitted to the corporation, their own design department has started to redesign major kitchen appliances with these five points in mind. They even formed a new division that dealt exclusively with the owners and managers of apartment blocks and condominiums. The public can now buy these energy efficient, long-lasting units by requesting a "Special Institutional Appliances Catalogue."

In the United States, latent product junkies first get hooked when they are still babies. Toddlers playing with shoddily made, badly designed toys learn that things exist to be thrown away and replaced by anything "new." They observe the way their parents deal with their own possessions.

There are many ways of developing a collector's instinct at an early age. Baseball cards are fairly innocent, but as children begin to collect, swap, trade, and buy, they learn that big business is more than ready to help with special albums, catalogues, and collecting trays. Children like to play with miniature automobiles, but it is only recently that collecting cases have been offered by Matchbox, Hot Wheels, Tonka, and other manufacturers. These small plastic dispatch cases are emblazoned with vaguely anthropomorphic hot rods, hold thirty-six, forty-eight, or seventy-two tiny cars, encouraging young collectors to buy more and more models. The same system is used to hook children on Mattel's Barbie Doll. She and her sidekicks, Ken and Skipper, are voracious 'consumers' of doll clothing, toy cars, play swimming pools, and other trashy accessories expertly copied from the equally worthless grown-up models.

Dollhouses are like regular homes—existing to store consumer goods. As in the real world, the dollhouse is relatively inexpensive when compared to what it holds. Dollhouse furnishings have become a thriving industry. There are tawdry, injection-molded forks, knives, and spoons—a table setting for four can cost up to $6. There is even a sterling silver table setting for dolly and her friends that sells for $125 a place setting. An astonishingly crude, slush-molded plastic pint-size piano made in Taiwan costs $7.98. A dollhouse concert grand that actually plays (and needs frequent tuning) costs $1,800. A 3½-inch tropical plant made of silk and standing in its own little pot sells for a dollar more than the real thing. Dollhouses have even been electrified. A do-it-yourself enthusiast owning a three-bedroom dollhouse must expect to spend about $150 to install a transformer, power lines, and tiny light bulbs. The newest wrinkle in dollhouse salesmanship is Lilliputian dollhouses with microscopic furnishings and furniture, which dollhouse owners can buy to put into their dollhouses for the dolls to play with!

There is nothing wrong with children playing with dollhouses, small cars, or baseball cards. What is disturbing is the hard-core advertising that uses these toys to encourage children to own, collect, and ultimately risk becoming product addicts.

The research on large kitchen appliances cited earlier attempted to cure product addiction by encouraging people to own less. We own many things that we could easily do without. Statistics have been assembled that show that in many parts of the United States, lawnmowers are used for an average of four hours a week. Snowblowers, even in the northernmost regions of the country, are used on an average of one hour a week.[4] Similar statistics can be provided for small electric hand tools and appliances. Sharing with others, co-ownership, renting, and leasing would all make a great deal more sense and would break the consumption cycle.

We are taught from the cradle to become product addicts, and unlike other human activities, it is a habit that endures beyond our death. Undertakers and morticians get one last grab at product junkies. The number of coffins, shrouds, winding sheets, pillows, pillowcases, and clothing manufactured specially for burial is staggering. When my mother died, some years ago, my initial meeting with the funeral director took place in his office, a plush room decorated with a large color photograph of eighty-six flag-draped coffins standing in neat rows in the sand. I asked him what this picture signified, and if his firm had been involved. "No," he said, "that was the Grand Canyon air disaster. We had nothing to do with it, but it was a triumph of our profession!" He then took me to his coffin showroom, a place curiously similar to a car showroom. Around thirty different coffins, ranging from $1,500 to $6,000 (in 1968) were on view. They were hideous beyond belief—plastic wraps in gold-anodized aluminum, wood-grain Formica laminated plastic, "silver" and "goldtone" handles and heavily embroidered polyester "satin look" pillows and sheets. Built-in cassette players played funeral music.

67

I explained that I wanted a simple oak box with an equally unadorned wooden cross on top. "Oh, you want *simple*," my funeral friend replied. "That's going to cost you plenty! Coffins like that have to be imported from Finland and run at $4,000 each." Five years later I was able to check the actual cost of such a coffin in Finland. It sold for $80.

From the cradle to the grave we are the victims of a system that hooks us into consumption patterns and product addiction. The danger lies not so much in the needless expense or the doomed effort to keep up with the Joneses, but in other areas. We are becoming alienated from many of the things that once gave us delight and nourishment. Our "spend more, buy more, consume more" society is based on a public whose tastes are constantly estranged from traditional concepts of excellence, and our acquisitive drives are completely unrestrained by notions of quality or excellence. Once taste is amputated from tradition it becomes the slave of fashion, and fashion is a puppet that dances to the tune of profit. If we are all turning into "competent consumers" (to use David Riesman's felicitous phrase)—mercurial, malleable, footloose, and easily persuadable—then this dangerous state of affairs is not only due to the Madison Avenue brigade, but also the virtuosos of production innovation.

The daily promptings of advertisers gradually make us believe that the only important things in life are the satisfactions money can buy. But as we slowly sink into a sewage of discarded products, all the gadgets of yesterday lie rotting on the landscape, poisoning the earth, the waters, and the heavens above.

Watching the trucks stream along the highways all over the country, one is tempted to believe that this is proof of our prosperity and economic strength. But the cargo includes frozen TV dinners, mascara dispensers, tranquilizers, video surveillance devices, trash compactors, and plastic flying ducks. The northern hemisphere produces and consumes more than all previous societies. This has been true since the time of colonialism. During the last thirty-five years, high technology and aggressive mass sales campaigns have continued this trend.

The consequences of continuous technological and design innovation are most severe in their influence on the relationships between people. Beyond basic survival standards, the roots of our tranquility and delight do not reside in the products we buy, but in such enduring things as the perception of beauty, friendship, loyalty, love, and a delight in excellence. The danger lies in the fact that we are taught to objectify our needs and, since sooner or later we become disenchanted with and alienated from the objects we buy, our real needs remain unfulfilled. In human terms, the result is destructive. In terms of shrinking resources and dwindling energy, it is a price that we can no longer afford to pay.

4
Simplification

It may be true that one has to choose between ethics and aesthetics, but it is no less true that whichever one chooses, one will always find the other at the end of the road.

JEAN-LUC GODARD

TWO hundred years ago, it was easy. The design of a tool, artifact, or transportation device, much like the design of a home or the pages of a book, followed rules that were easy to understand by designer, architect, and public alike. It was commonly accepted by designers, their critics and their audience that:

1. Design should show how a tool was used and what it was used for.

2. The finished product should express the materials, tools, and processes used in its manufacture.

3. The product, object, or artifact should work well with a minimum of repair or maintenance.

4. The designed object should meet the expectations of the end users.

5. Most things should be made at the direct request of the people, to fulfill a specific need or want.

Until around 200 years ago, the technological function of products was visible and could be easily understood. To have someone make you a dining table of yellow deal or a pitcher of porcelain or pewter was a transaction that involved both the craftsman and the customer.

There were, of course, more sophisticated devices. Pocket watches, Amati violins, printing presses, Jacquard looms, Tennessee squirrel rifles, navigational sextants, and New Bedford clipper ships all come to mind. But even Thomas Wainbright, "philosophical instrument maker" at Sevendials in London, received his orders from people thoroughly conversant with both the limitations of his craft and their own needs.

Our tools have become increasingly complex. An army of middlemen has positioned itself between those who design and build and those who use and buy. Many of the instructions for tools we currently use are difficult to understand even by experts. From the late 1920s to the mid-1930s, industrial designers found themselves faced with machinery whose function could no longer be derived visually through common sense or logic, and began encasing these constructs in so-called shrouds. A method or work that no longer made sense was tucked away behind metal or wooden covers. This shrouding performed a secondary and equally important job—it protected delicate engine parts from dust and other contamination. In the 1970s, chip technology, minicomputers, and microprocessors emerged as small, black-box concepts, which many users did not understand. Linked to this, extreme microminiaturization and a wealth of new materials have made it possible for designers and manufacturers to "make anything look like anything we want, make anything look like something else."[1]

With the introduction of completely new devices in the marketplace, the concept of product identity has become an important element of design. We have electric razors that look like small transistor radios (and vice versa), remote controls for television sets and stereos that look like calculators, and microwave ovens that look like television sets at ten paces. This list grows daily. In his article "After Modernism: Towards a New Industrial Design Aesthetic" as well as during some speeches Mark Brutton, former editor of the British magazine *Design*, raised provoking and disturbing questions about "what things should look like in general," now that chip technology and microprocessors are so small that literally any shape can be adopted for anything. Brutton implied that the electronic and plastic possibilities leading to an unlimited choice in form may lead to a new age of product styling, a re-emergence of appearance design.[2]

There is no question that the growing use of microprocessors and minichips is changing the products we use in a number of curious ways. At the time of writing it is already possible to purchase an automobile that, according to the manufacturers, not only provides an "inboard computer readout" giving data on gas consumption, oil pressure, average driving speed, expected time of arrival and engine temperature. It even tells the driver these things in "a pleasant baritone voice." Microwave ovens, clothes dryers, and a good many other appliances will soon be chattering to us, giving us bits of information, and generally cluttering up our auditory environment. Six-hundred extra dollars for a box screwed to the dashboard of a Cadillac may seem little enough at today's inflated prices, but it adds more complexity, more things that can go wrong. In no way does it help the car to perform better. (On the other hand, recent developments have used computer chips in cars to help improve fuel-injection performance and tell the driver the optimum time to shift.) By phasing out old products and pushing the latest technological gimmicks (whether they make sense or not), we are losing many good designs of the past. A simple example will suffice.

Toasters are small electrical appliances used by most of us. The first thing that usually goes wrong with a toaster is the warning light and the color sensor that tells us when the toast is the right shade of brown. The next thing to go is the timer switch. After that, especially if thick pieces of French bread have been forced into the slits, the pop-up feature breaks down. The electric-cord attachment is the next trouble spot. After that, the sides discolor and tarnish and the plastic edging chips. Toasters are expensive and difficult to get repaired, so eventually we usually throw them away and buy a new one.

Simplifying a design can sometimes mean going back to the past. Figure 4-1 shows a used toaster I bought for less than a dollar. It is electric and is working well in its seventy-fifth year. The sides have to be flipped open by hand and are designed so that when they are reclosed they flip the piece of bread over. There are no timers, lights, switches, or anything else that can go wrong. The power cord attaches separately, eliminating another trouble area. The user must check to see that the toast does not burn, but this is made up for by the fact that the four heating coils that power this low-energy toaster can be easily replaced by the owner. In addition, the top of the toaster has been designed to keep bread warm. I feel fully confident that when I die I can

Figure 4-1. *Designed and manufactured in the United States, this electric toaster dates back to 1906 and is still being used. Author's collection. (Photograph by Paul Wise)*

leave the toaster to my daughter and that it will still be performing well in its hundredth year.

The statement "They don't make things the way they used to" no longer elicits a smirk. Instead it is greeted with wholehearted agreement.

Design must never be intrusive, yet current mass marketing techniques ensure that it is. Stoves, for example, are designed to stand next to one another in retail shops and discount stores screaming their superiority over competing brands. This visual manipulation is achieved through surface styling, which means that once the appliance is installed in the home, instead of receding into decent anonymity, it continues, aesthetically and visually, to scream.

In the design of high-fidelity components, sanity has been long overdue. Bang & Olufsen have designed sets (figure 4-2) that manage to disappear visually. The manufacturers obviously believe that a maze of lights, toggle switches, meters, and knobs is not

Figure 4-2. *The Bang & Olufsen high fidelity set. Designed and manufactured in Denmark. (Photograph courtesy of Bang & Olufsen, Denmark)*

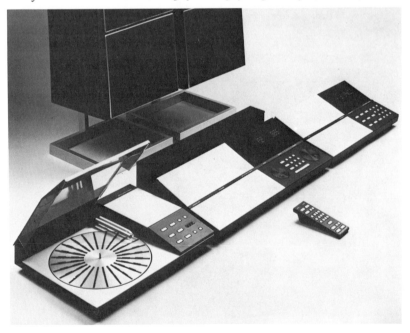

necessary for the functioning of their sets, and are merely merchandising gimmicks. One of their sets uses a cigarette-pack-sized remote control unit to switch channels, select volume, and balance the speakers. It is not linked to the rest of the system through wiring, and it provides splendid acoustic fidelity without any "sexing up" of its appearance. Significantly, the set does not sell well in the United States. As someone in their marketing department commented, "Americans won't spend $6,000 for high fidelity that is simple and disappears visually."

The German electronics and radio firm, Uher, developed their Miniset several years ago (figure 4-3). It is ultracompact, with three components: and AM/FM tuner with digital station readout, a master control with amplifiers and preamplifiers, and a com-

Figure 4-3. Hi-Fi Miniset *by Uher of Germany. One of the first ultraminiaturized high fidelity sound systems that offers reproduction qualities* exceeding *those of the large, bloated, chrome-encrusted boxes most people have become used to. Note small box of wooden matches to indicate size of unit. Author's collection. (Photograph courtesy of Uher GmBH, Munich, West Germany)*

bination portable cassette player and recorder. When stacked together, the components are smaller than an unabridged dictionary. The quality of the Miniset's sound reproduction is among the best in the world, but the set does not sell well in the United States for the same reason that Bang & Olufsen's products do not. The set is fairly expensive and European marketing experts suggest that when Americans spend a lot of money, they want to flaunt what they have bought.

The flaunting is where the trouble comes in. It is one thing to style a tool or product so that its appearance is a crisp and lucid accompaniment to its purpose. It is quite another to make the ornamentation as important as the function itself. And it is inexcusable for the embellishment to interfere with the working of the object. Technics, a division of Panasonic, has recently introduced a high fidelity turntable precisely the size of a record jacket. Sales in Japan and northern Europe have been substantial, but in the United States the unit has been largely rejected because "it looks too small, simple and inconsequential for $750."[3]

An analogy can be drawn here with abnormal sexual behavior, specifically with fetishism. Sex is a joyful and affirmative act. Some people may be excited by a specific piece of their loved one's clothing, and certain items, a lacy undergarment for example, may even enhance their sexual pleasure. But if a person begins to fixate all of his sexual desires on lace underwear, then the sexual symbol has replaced the love act, and has become an end in itself. In the same way many of us substitute an object's appearance for its fundamental purpose.

Mankind has always used decoration, embellishment and ornamentation on tools, objects and possessions. Primitive spears and harpoons were frequently carved with naturalistic pictures of the animals to be hunted. During the Middle Ages, a nobleman's coat of arms appear with monotonous regularity on his shield, carriage, banners, and household silver, while equally ubiquitous chrysanthemums and linked cherry blossoms gleamed on the sedan chairs, sword guards, and kimonos of his Japanese counterpart. But labeling things with words and slogans, identifying them in a nonpersonalized way, is something relatively new. We have changed our basic approach. We no longer use labels to personalize objects, to make them our own. We now use nameplates to depersonalize our goods, to declare that they are just like everyone else's.

It is becoming difficult to buy a plain canvas carryall without such slogans such as "Pepsi Generation," "Conserve Energy," or that does not display portraits of Big Bird or Kliban's cats. Along with the stencilled grins of Garfield the cat, E.T., and Linus, these logos are becoming a sort of visual Muzak.

Luggage seems especially subject to this slogan mania. When flying back from Brazil recently, I observed an otherwise normal looking woman carrying a garment bag and three smaller bags, all made of handsome cotton canvas. The garment bag had "Glad Rags" printed on it in 6-inch eggplant-colored letters, and "Shoesies," "Stuff," and "Dirty Dainties" appeared on the remaining pieces of the ensemble. Why?

Part of the reason is, that as quality becomes more rare, we are using decoration to fill the void. We hope that boring products will somehow be magically transformed if we print the cynical advertising slogan of some company or the facile grin of some popular personality across their surface.

The advantages of unobtrusive design are complex and difficult to explain. An example from interior design may serve to make the point. Imagine a simple workroom, its walls and ceiling painted flat white. Then imagine an 8-inch pipe running from floor to ceiling in one corner of the room. The problem? How to deal with the pipe visually. Here are seven possibilities:

1. A square box in natural wood could be built around the pipe (figure 4-4). This would provide an "excuse" for the pipe by disguising it as a structural support. This is an awkward solution, making the pipe into something it is not.

2. We could paint the pipe with fake woodgrain to make it look like a tree trunk (figure 4-5). Here we're implying a different material, and are getting involved in a conceptual lie, as in the first instance.

3. The pipe could be painted survival orange or bright red for the greatest possible contrast (figure 4-6). It would then com-

Figure 4-4. *The triumph of fake: the pipe has been enclosed in a false wooden beam.*

Figure 4-5. *We can paint the pipe to look like a Greek column or put a fraudulent wood-grain design on it and hope it will look like a tree.*

Figure 4-6. *The pipe could be painted bright survival orange to really stand out or in a gentle pastel color for slightly less contrast.*

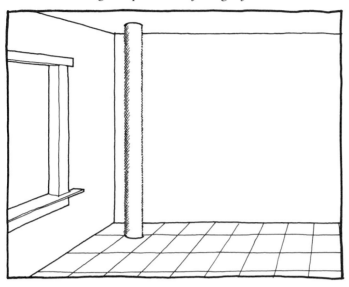

Figure 4-7. *High-tech: Watching raw sewage float through the room in a clear pipe seems to delight some architects.*

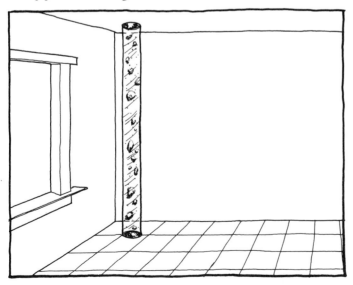

municate great contrast, possibly danger, which would be appropriate if steam or hot water were carried through the pipe.

4. It could be painted in a pastel yellow, green, pink, or blue, but this would be fudging the issue. This solution is purely decorative, and like the survival orange version, would make the pipe visually important.

5. The pipe could be clear plastic (figure 4-7), but having watched table scraps float unappetizingly through such a conduit in a contemporary villa in Milan, I find this solution unpalatable.

6. The pipe could be buried in the wall (figure 4-8). This would make it invisible, but would be expensive to install or repair.

7. Finally, the designer could paint the pipe the same white as the walls (figure 4-9). This would diminish the difference between the two elements. The pipe would still be there, but would visually recede. This is by far the cheapest and most elegant solution. It is a simple matter of contrast versus harmony. Although contrast can be pleasing, in the example given it seems clear that visual disappearance should be effected.

Simplification leads to elegance. Simplification also implies common sense, a quality that seems to get rarer as the world becomes bureaucratized. Elegance as I use the word here means that a problem has been solved directly, un-self-consciously, with minimal effort and in such a way that the object or product can be understood easily and is a good fit with its environment. Designers, architects, and planners seek order. They try to make sense out of chaos, to bring direction to what is not yet formed. This implies a *search for good form*, the basic pattern-seeking, pattern-generating need that lies at the base of all human thought and action. Some experiments may make this point more clearly.

The psychological mechanism at the base of our search for form is called *closure*. When presented with a diagram of three dots in space (figure 4-10), or with three V-shaped figures (figure 4-11), most people will establish closure between the three groups and manage to see a triangle. When presented with a senseless blob (figure 4-12), most people will again pull this shape into a triangular form that "makes sense." This has been established by

Figure 4-8. *A "best" solution: The pipe is really invisible since it has been buried in the wall. In case of trouble, very expensive to repair and maintain.*

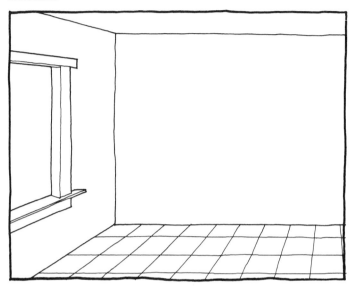

Figure 4-9. *Elegant, unobtrusive, simple, and cheap. The pipe is the same white as the walls and recedes visually.*

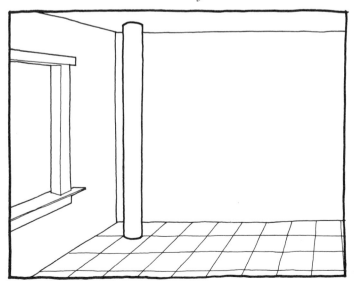

•

Figure 4-10. *Three dots in space forming a triangle in the viewer's mind through "closure."*

•   •

Figure 4-11. *Three V-shapes ease the process of closure for the viewer.*

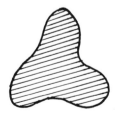

Figure 4-12. *An equilateral triangle that has been manipulated to form a senseless blob.*

psychologists. The psychological mechanism has been called "the search for good form."

With this in mind, twenty-one years ago I developed two experiments to prove to my students and myself that the search for good form is a reality for all of us. I have carried out this experiment twice a year ever since, testing between thirty and sixty subjects each time, meaning that nearly 3,000 young people have participated in the experiment. The experiment involved students from eleven countries: Denmark; Finland; Sweden; Austria; Australia; Papua New Guinea; Nigeria; Brazil; Great Britain; Canada; and the United States.

The students were shown two simple designs (figures 4-13 and 4-14). The reader will notice that in the second drawing the figure is intentionally labeled A-B-M-D. After presenting the two designs to the group, the designs were wiped off the board and each student was asked to draw both pictures from memory, making no notes of them in his or her notebook and handing in the results immediately. The students' drawings were then destroyed at once. A week later, the students were asked to produce the drawings again, this time from memory, and to hand them in at once, whereupon the drawings were once again destroyed. This process was repeated once a week for fifteen weeks.

At the end of the fifteen-week testing period, the first drawing looked like a large asterisk in 91% of the drawings (figure 4-15). In 54% of the cases, the second drawing had been evened out and relabeled A-B-C-D (figure 4-16). In 41% of the drawings of the second design, the right leg had been even further exaggerated than in the original and had been relabeled A-B-X-D (figure 4-17).

The basic drawing and thinking mechanisms are easy to explain. Tiny mistakes caused by "misremembering" the original design and sloppy drawing crept in week by week. These errors were cumulative and finally resulted in the drawings shown. It will be noted, however, that all of the drawing mistakes, all of the memory lapses, and all of the cumulative errors moved toward identical images in more than 90% of the cases.

What do the new figures have in common? The first design, the asterisk, is probably the only sensible form that can emerge from the scattered hen tracks that formed the starting image. In

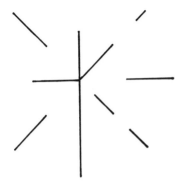

Figure 4-13. *Test Figure 1: the incomplete asterisk.*

Figure 4-14. *Test Figure 2: the apparently arbitrary diagram A-B-M-D.*

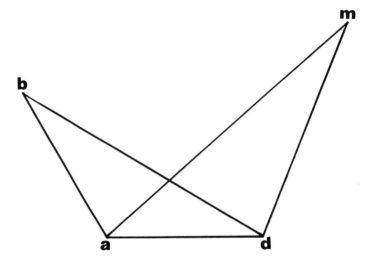

the second original image, the intent of the designer is unclear. The design seems out of balance and the labeling is nonsense. In this case, more than half of the students have decided (on an unconscious level) to regularize the picture and relabel it the way "it ought to be."

Slightly less than half the students chose (again unconsciously) to remember the original visual imbalance, resulting in a wildly exaggerated right leg. Although they remembered that the odd leg was marked differently, they have chosen to relabel it X, because X stands for the unknown in most equations, and because

M does not make sense mathematically or geometrically in the context. In all three cases, the participants have unknowingly pursued a search for good form, for something that makes sense, something that is easy to remember—an emblematic device.

This basic experiment comes to grips with perceptual factors in terms of Gestalt psychology and should influence designers' search for consistent form. Common sense must prevail when a design is planned.[4]

The design profession is beset with professional jargon and working procedures that are confusing to the uninitiated. For example, assume that we are building a thirty-foot square swimming pool, edged with a two-foot concrete walk. On each of the four sides, three poplars, about 12-feet tall, are to be planted at precise intervals. To communicate the appearance of all this visually usually calls for a perspective sketch (figure 4-18). But when looking at the sketch, we see that it does not provide any information about sizes, the placement of the trees, or other important details. Either this information must be dimensioned in separately, or specifications must accompany the drawing. Many laymen will not understand the drawing at all, and to some it may communicate

Figure 4-15. *Test Figure 1: After fifteen weeks the asterisk magically completes itself in 91% of all drawings.*

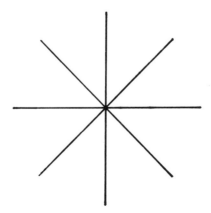

Figure 4-16. *Test Figure 2, first variation: After fifteen weeks, 54% of all students have now "evened out" the diagram and relabeled it A-B-C-D.*

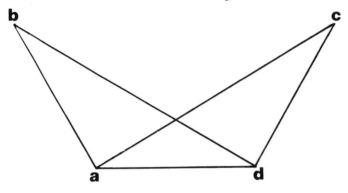

Figure 4-17. *In 41% of the drawings students have exaggerated the meaningless aspects of the design and relabeled it A-B-X-D.*

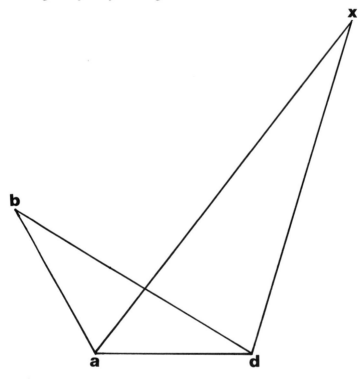

Figure 4-18. *A conventional perspective drawing of the swimming pool and the trees that surround it. (Drawing by Barry Crone)*

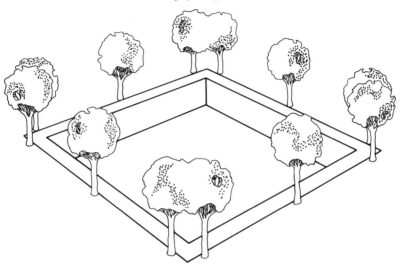

chaos. Some people when shown the sketch said, "But I thought all the trees were supposed to be the same height—the ones in the back look shorter," or, "Look—the trees are growing into each other!" Some said with alarm, "I thought the pool was square, not that funny rhomboid shape!"

It is easy to say that people do not understand because they do not know how to look at perspective drawings. Or that people are not used to seeing perspectives that shows things the way they really are. Yet nothing could be further from the truth. The rendering shows the pool and the trees as they might look to a person in a helicopter, hovering forty-five feet above ground, fifty feet from the front edge of the pool.

Perspective is just one version of reality. It is an artistic convention and no more.

The same pool and trees are shown as they appeared in a Coptic manuscript (figure 4-19). Here everything is measurable. The pool is the right size and shape and the trees are equidistant and the right height. All the relationships are precise and to scale. If you argue that the trees seem to be lying down, you are merely showing that you are accustomed to the conventions of perspective drawings.

Of course, designers and architects use a number of supplemental drawings—sections, details, call-outs, exploded views, and straight orthographic projections. But in the case of the swimming pool, the modest Coptic drawing communicates everything, and is easiest to understand by those who are not accustomed to designer short-hand. This is not an argument for doing away with perspective, but a plea for fitting the message to the audience.

Figure 4-19. *The same pool and trees, as they would appear in a Coptic manuscript. (Drawing by Barry Crone)*

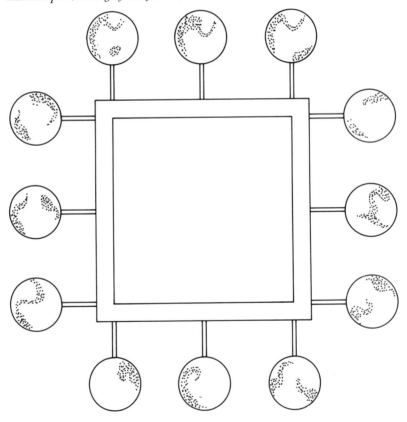

One of the basic functions of good graphic design is to make words and images understandable. Because my lectures involve traveling to many countries, I have frequently found myself in a strange city, trapped in a taxi with a driver unable to find my destination. He usually whips out a city map and an enormous magnifying glass in a desperate attempt to find the right address. Often he ends up handing both map and magnifier to me. In the swaying cab I then indulge in a frenzied search, trying to distinguish *"Nevsky Prospekt"* from *"Alexandrov Ul."*

The print is usually too small. The print on most charts, maps, technical literature, and packaging is frequently difficult to read for anyone with vision less than perfect vision. Remarkably, medicine labels usually show the name of the pharmaceutical company and drugstore in large bright letters, while the side effects and cautionary warnings are in minuscule type. One item in my collection has yellow typeface on a white background, making the words virtually invisible.

Simplicity and common sense seem to be curiously absent in design. One of the tasks of architects and designers is to make things simple without making them simplistic. In an increasingly complex world, cluttered by enigmatic messages, perplexing tools, and cryptic objects, the designer's task is to unravel the Gordian knot of confusion and help express things clearly and simply.

5
Humanization of Design

Virtually everything that works today began with a vision, and with a group of idealists prepared to work for it.

BARBARA WARD

T HE function of architects and designers can be variously defined as problem seeking, problem solving, and decision making. Apologists for the design and architecture establishment insist on a success rate of nearly 100%, and the statistic is true depending on how you judge the results. Even the original premise, that the designer solves problems, is valid.

But the real question should be: just what kind of problems do designers solve with such routinely perfect success rates? The problems that designers solve in the real world are those they have posed for themselves or those that have been posed for them by industry. In other words, if I invent a problem and then set about answering it, the answer may be new, beguiling, creative, and even worthwhile. But when all is said and done the challenge, which has been so cleverly answered, did not exist to begin with. It was a problem specifically created to be solved.

Remember that needs arise from people, not from the heads of designers or from corporate decision makers. When the wrong problems are set, the wrong solutions emerge. Frequently these solutions are dehumanizing, demeaning, and highly mechanistic. The products we use, the cars we drive, and the buildings we live and work in often lack a human face.

It would be understandable if this discrepancy between what is needed and what is supplied were unique to capitalist countries, but design with a human face is also lacking in the Soviet-bloc nations, Cuba, and the People's Republic of China. And although young romantics in developing countries have tried to endow design with all the noble savagery of Rousseau, the same mechanistic and technocratic values are appearing in the third world. Even the 'dropout' communes, which proliferated like mushrooms in the late 1960s and early 1970s, presented a dubious mixture of Stone Age living standards and high technology. The humanization of design is probably the single most important task facing designers and architects today. It depends on consultation with people, rigorous but sensitive simplification, minimal intervention whenever possible, and sturdy common sense.

It could be argued that most of the consumer products designed in the last ten years—riding lawnmowers, twenty-six-inch color televisions, snowmobiles, sports cars, electric pasta makers—are really adult toys. We can see a new threat emerging: the subservience of people to machines. This hideous direction is most clearly seen when looking at children's toys, especially Christmas offerings. (Can you remember when the most important Christmas question was not: "Do I have enough batteries?")

One of the best-selling Christmas dolls recently was a little battery-driven dog that urinates on a small newspaper. Electronic games, costing $29.95 and sardonically called Football, Hockey, and Baseball, provide specious amusement, issuing shrill buzzing sounds and eating up batteries at an alarming rate. *Four billion dollars* are now netted by the home video industry: The idiot box has become a twenty-first century pinball arcade (it is interesting to note in this connection that recent consumer reports indicate that color TV sets more than ten-years-old emit hard radiation which is especially harmful to children under twelve playing video games, since they are much too close to the set). One can buy more elaborate items such as an electronic version of a chess game (figure 5-1). Looking like a cross between Han Solo's laser gun and a pinball machine, it has winking, blinking lights and a limited vocabulary. What's wrong with the *real* chess? It is a wonderful game—educational and a lot of fun. And compared to its microprocessed sibling, dirt cheap. Although computerized chess games are programmed to beat all but the best players, the tactile and visual satisfaction of handling *real* pieces, as well as dealing with a real live opponent are missing.

These electronic stocking stuffers have five things in common:

1. They all look like the offspring of an unholy union between Battlestar Galactica and a 1962 Cadillac.

2. They are made of cheap, brittle plastic that chips and cracks easily and comes in a dreadful range of colors.

3. They do only one thing and they do it badly.

Figure 5-1. *An electronic chess game with a hydraulic arm to move the pieces.*

4. They devour expensive batteries the way a one-armed bandit guzzles quarters.

5. While there seems to be a need for this electronic rubbish (all of the games make highly acceptable last-minute Christmas gifts), nevertheless I have observed these gadgets in use, and for most children the novelty wears off after a few days or weeks.

But there is a darker side to all of this. Can you remember sitting around the kitchen table playing Monopoly? Do you recall playing touch football? Think of long brooding hours playing chess against a human opponent rather than a preprogrammed computer. How about the satisfactory click of dominoes (see figure 5–2) on the parlor table?

All of the computerized, microminiaturized, microprocessed toys that beep, gurgle, wheeze, and wink make playtime an intensely *private* time—they wrap the child in a buzzing, clicking cocoon with flickering idiot lights. The child becomes an only child, a temporary orphan, cut off from friends and parents. Child psychologists who receive princely retainers from the toy industry to endorse anything that sells, tell us that these games

Figure 5-2. *Maybe the Japanese understanding of good design comes from playing Go. Any designer would consider the arrangement of black and white counters on this board to be superbly "good design." Note that the game is played by hand, not electronically. The thickness of the Go-board gives a different clicking sound to the pieces. This sound communicates to spectators the degree of skill the owner of the board has achieved. (Photograph by John Charlton)*

"teach the child to interface with the machine." This is not only rotten English, but it is even worse psychology.

Why not let the machine relate to the child instead? Why not design machines that relate to people rather than the other way around? This has been achieved intelligently and with sensitivity with electronic teaching aids. Some teaching machines relate to the specific strengths, weaknesses, and rates of progress of the children they are teaching. Texas Instruments' Little Professor game is one example. It notes the number of mistakes the child makes and lowers the level of difficulty accordingly. As the child improves, the level is increased again. Learning through play is the best way for children to learn with commitment. The designers and manufacturers of electronic toys and games could learn from the design of computerized learning games.

A good example of the lack of common sense in design is the drawer pull. The primary function of a drawer pull is to ensure that a drawer can be pulled out with a minimum of effort. Its secondary function is to protect the hand from injury and keep the front of the cabinet clean.

Historically, the first drawer knobs were round wooden buttons (figure 5-3). But because lathe-turned wooden objects tend to show a great deal of end grain and, at the same time, are handled more and subjected to greater stress than the front fascia of the drawer itself, these knobs tended to discolor and split easily. For this reason, round white porcelain knobs (figure 5-4) became the norm around 1700 and were commonly used in the United States from colonial times to the late nineteenth century. Porcelain knobs were easy to clean, pleasant to handle, and did not splinter or split like their wooden predecessors.

At the end of the nineteenth century, drawer pulls appeared in the shapes of acanthus leaves, swans, and a plethora of meaningless curlicues, scrolls, and flower petals (figures 5-5 and 5-6). In North America, the popularity of this style has not waned.

Finnish and Danish designers have developed the simple drawer pull shown in figure 5-7. It is made of heavy-gauge wire approximately three-inches wide and two-inches deep and is finished in stainless steel, brass, brushed aluminum, or a variety of bright primary colors. The handle works well and by projecting at least

94

Figure 5-3. *Wooden drawer knobs. (Photograph by John Charlton)*

Figure 5-4. *White china knobs.* *(Photograph by John Charlton)*

Figure 5-5. *Flourishes and dust catchers designed in the United States, 1977. (Photograph by John Charlton)*

Figure 5-6. *Metal inset door handles on Japanese* tansu *chest. Meiji period, author's collection. (Photograph by John Charlton)*

Figure 5-7. *A well-designed cabinet handle from northern Europe. (Photograph by John Charlton)*

two inches from drawer front, it provides good leverage so that people do not bruise their knuckles against the cabinet. The point of the story is that during the last three years, American manufacturers and their subsidiaries in Taiwan and Korea have provided cheap copies of these handles for the North American market. But the design adaptation has been done with a minimum of common sense and no thought for ergonomics. These rip-offs are less than 1¼-inches deep, meaning insufficient clearance between the cabinet front and the handle and banged knuckles. Furthermore, in making the fixture less expensive, the diameter of the wire has been reduced from a robust half inch to a thin, emaciated wire.

The humanization of design implies examining the original design brief and then listing all of the necessary or desirable aspects that are lacking. Design analysis helps to restate the brief and provide specific goals and directions for the design.

Bepla/Planet Products Pty. is an Australian firm that produces task lights called Planet for the office, home, and public spaces. I was asked to develop a newer version of their best-selling desk lamp. This lamp had been designed in the mid-1960s, had received the Australian Design Award, and had been marketed with enormous success in Australia, New Zealand and other parts of Southeast Asia. Below is an excerpt from the design brief:

Redesign of Studio "C" Lamp:

The Studio "C" Lamp has sold well for about fifteen years. The adjustable swinging arms, various attachment methods to desk or table, and many different bases have now been consumer tested through actual use for a decade and a half.

The following points should be taken into consideration in redesigning the lamp:

A. Consumer complaints are very few. The only irritation expressed has to do with the fact that the head (shade) of the lamp becomes very warm, sometimes too hot to be touched. *Redesign.*

B. The shape of the head, commonly referred to as "bullet-shade" has become a visual cliché, it is dated looking, has a fiftyish appearance, and—at the same time—seems very technocratic. *Redesign.*

C. Explore how the head can be redesigned to bring about a more positive visual value. *Rethink.*

D. Is it possible to provide more light (more lumens) with the same wattage, or lower wattage bulbs and save electric costs? *Research and rethink.*

After consulting with workers and management at Bepla/Planet Products Pty. users were also brought into the discussion. As in any other similar design job, materials, manufacturing processes available at the factory, and marketing logistics were investigated. This led to a restatement of the design brief.

I decided to let the new design flow directly from the new shade, retaining the successful and popular arms and bases. The result was the new Studio Greenshade lamp (figures 5-8 and

Figure 5-8. *The studio "Greenshade" lamp, showing double paraboloid reflector. Designed for Planet Products Pty. by the author.* (Photograph by Paul Wise)

5-9). The spun green metal shade is familiar from turn-of-the-century bookkeeper's desks and poker tables, but the lamp is more than just a nostalgic restatement. The design helps to give the lamp a human feel. It is also more than just another articulated desk lamp. Careful design of the shade, as well as a built-in, stringently calculated parabolic clip-on reflector, makes it possible to cut down on energy usage. A 25-watt bulb will give a light output equivalent to 60 watts, a 40-watt bulb will approach a 100-watt output. The redesigned shade, together with the parabolic reflector, maintains a low temperature, which not only prevents people from burning themselves, but also extends bulb life.

Minimal design intervention, the other leg on which our case for the humanization of design rests, means working with sensitivity, modesty, and frugality and in close cooperation with users and workers. An example deals with the beating of maize, corn, and other cereals. This separates flour and vegetable oils from the chaff and husks. In many developing countries, this work is performed by women and young boys who spend eight or nine hours a day, day after day, flailing the cereal with sticks (figure 5-10). It is a back-breaking job.

Figure 5-9. *Second view of the "Greenshade" lamp.*
(Photograph by Paul Wise)

Figure 5-10. *Flailing cereals in Tanzania.*

The Taiwanese have developed a handy little electronic grain-grinder to help with this problem. However, there are some difficulties. Most villages in the bush have no electricity. If they do, they do not have the cash to import expensive electric gadgets. But even if electricity and cash were available, the Chinese model would grind the entire tribe's harvest in two or three minutes, thus destroying an important social grouping.

Christine Lock, a postgraduate student from Britain, decided that she had an obligation as a designer to help with minimum intervention. Instead of designing and building yet another grain mill, she developed a sketch book, a bit like a *Whole Earth Catalogue*, containing hundreds of simple blow-apart sketches of primitive grinding devices used historically all over the world (figures 5-11 to 5-14). She printed several hundred copies and mailed them to people in third world countries.[1] The result, ten years later, is that nearly eighty people in different developing countries are designing their own unique hand grinders, each developed

Figure 5-11. *Material from the book on building a grain grinder. Designed, drawn, and developed by Christine Lock, as a postgraduate student of the author's at the Royal Academy of Architecture in Copenhagen.*

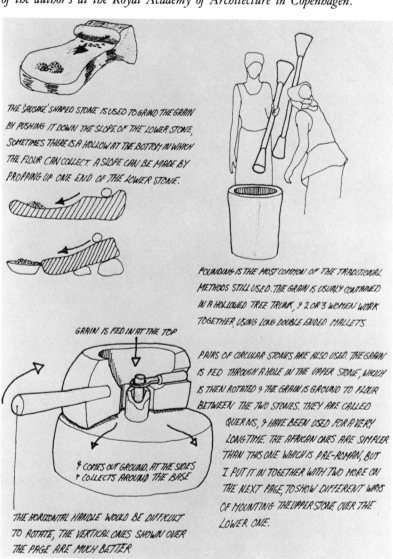

THE SAUSAGE SHAPED STONE IS USED TO GRIND THE GRAIN BY PUSHING IT DOWN THE SLOPE OF THE LOWER STONE, SOMETIMES THERE IS A HOLLOW AT THE BOTTOM IN WHICH THE FLOUR CAN COLLECT. A SLOPE CAN BE MADE BY PROPPING UP ONE END OF THE LOWER STONE.

POUNDING IS THE MOST COMMON OF THE TRADITIONAL METHODS STILL USED. THE GRAIN IS USUALLY CONTAINED IN A HOLLOWED TREE TRUNK, 9 2 OR 3 WOMEN WORK TOGETHER, USING LONG DOUBLE ENDED MALLETS

GRAIN IS FED IN AT THE TOP

PAIRS OF CIRCULAR STONES ARE ALSO USED. THE GRAIN IS FED THROUGH A HOLE IN THE UPPER STONE, WHICH IS THEN ROTATED 9 THE GRAIN IS GROUND TO FLOUR BETWEEN THE TWO STONES. THEY ARE CALLED QUERNS, 9 HAVE BEEN USED FOR A VERY LONG TIME. THE AFRICAN ONES ARE SIMPLER THAN THIS ONE WHICH IS PRE-ROMAN, BUT I PUT IT IN TOGETHER WITH TWO MORE ON THE NEXT PAGE, TO SHOW DIFFERENT WAYS OF MOUNTING THE UPPER STONE OVER THE LOWER ONE.

9 COMES OUT GROUND, AT THE SIDES 9 COLLECTS AROUND THE BASE

THE HORIZONTAL HANDLE WOULD BE DIFFICULT TO ROTATE, THE VERTICAL ONES SHOWN OVER THE PAGE ARE MUCH BETTER

Figure 5-12. *Material from the book on building a grain grinder. Designed, drawn, and developed by Christine Lock.*

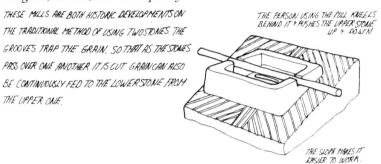

THESE MILLS ARE BOTH HISTORIC DEVELOPMENTS ON THE TRADITIONAL METHOD OF USING TWO STONES. THE GROOVES TRAP THE GRAIN, SO THAT AS THE STONES PASS OVER ONE ANOTHER IT IS CUT. GRAIN CAN ALSO BE CONTINUOUSLY FED TO THE LOWER STONE FROM THE UPPER ONE.

THE PERSON USING THE MILL KNEELS BEHIND IT & PUSHES THE UPPER STONE UP & DOWN

THE SLOPE MAKES IT EASIER TO WORK.

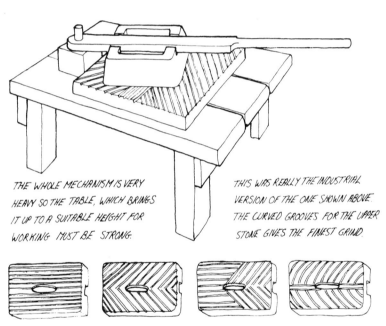

THE WHOLE MECHANISM IS VERY HEAVY SO THE TABLE, WHICH BRINGS IT UP TO A SUITABLE HEIGHT FOR WORKING MUST BE STRONG.

THIS WAS REALLY THE INDUSTRIAL VERSION OF THE ONE SHOWN ABOVE. THE CURVED GROOVES FOR THE UPPER STONE GIVES THE FINEST GRIND.

. 4 DIFFERENT WAYS OF CUTTING THE UNDERSIDE OF THE UPPER STONE.

Figure 5-13. *Material from the book on building a grain grinder. Designed, drawn, and developed by Christine Lock.*

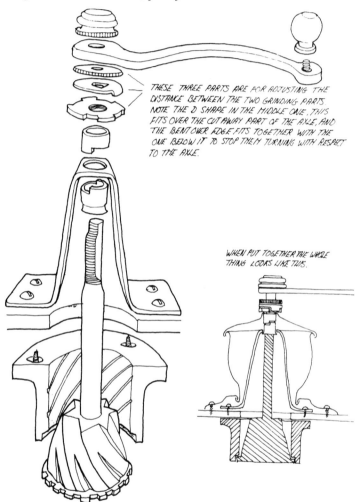

THESE THREE PARTS ARE FOR ADJUSTING THE
DISTANCE BETWEEN THE TWO GRINDING PARTS.
NOTE THE D SHAPE IN THE MIDDLE ONE, THIS
FITS OVER THE CUT AWAY PART OF THE AXLE, AND
THE BENT OVER EDGE FITS TOGETHER WITH THE
ONE BELOW IT TO STOP THEM TURNING WITH RESPECT
TO THE AXLE.

WHEN PUT TOGETHER THE WHOLE
THING LOOKS LIKE THIS.

INSTEAD OF USING A BRACKET & CENTERING PIN, THE DIAMETER OF THE BASE OF THE INNER
GRINDING PART HAS BEEN INCREASED, AND THE OUTER PART HAS BEEN STEPPED. THE 'TEETH'
PROVIDE GAPS TO LET THE GROUND COFFEE OUT. THE DRAWING IS ABOUT FULL SIZE.

Figure 5-14. *Material from the book on building a grain grinder. Designed, drawn, and developed by Christine Lock.*

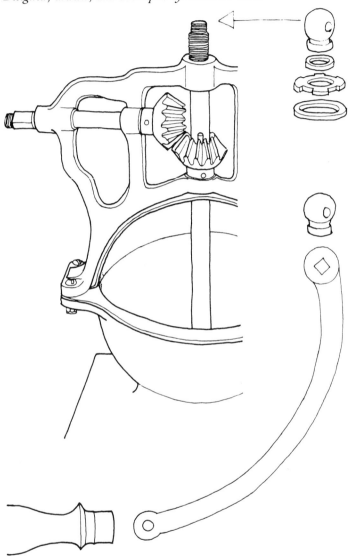

for the specific harvests, materials, and social working mores of the country in question. Minimum intervention encouraged a design that works in human terms. The social grouping that helps bind the tribe together, will continue to flourish. Instead of imposing a solution from outside, invention, innovation, and design have been returned to the people.

Nearly ten years ago, I worked with a Guatemalan postgraduate student in California. His parents owned a coffee plantation and had found that using small vans and trucks to harvest the coffee crop brought about serious ecological problems. Coffee plants are unusually susceptible to the pollution produced by internal-combustion engines. Hence, John Koester developed a muscle-powered truck to keep emission fumes away from the areas where the coffee was grown.

The vehicle (figure 5-15) could carry both the weight of the man pedaling it and a payload of 450 pounds over relatively uneven terrain. With two people pedaling, it could carry their weight and about 750 pounds. It can be seen that this muscle-powered truck is an odd collection of bicycle parts, derrailleur gears, motorcycle parts, golf-cart wheels and square tubing. The vehicle was specifically designed for decentralized modes of production. No factory manufactures it. Instead it is made by dozens of small bicycle shops in the countryside. This system enables each user to have his truck customized according to need. The truck can be gearless, can have three-speed Sturmy Archer gears, or ten- and fifteen-speed derrailleurs. Approximately 6,000 of these trucks have been built in Guatemala and Cuba. Because Papua New Guinea also has an excellent coffee crop, investigation is now going on to see if these bicycle trucks can be manufactured on a decentralized basis in that country.

A lot of children's furniture, baby furnishings, and other appliances for infants are designed for the grandparent market. Manufacturers state this quite frankly. There is more money to be made selling things to fond grandparents than to young parents. This market manipulation increases prices drastically. It gives rise to a bewildering array of appliances and constructions that make little or no sense and are impractical in daily family use.

Figure 5-15. *The all-terrain, muscle-powered truck for coffee plantations in Guatemala. Designed by J. Koester, a Guatemalan postgraduate student at the California Institute of the Arts.*

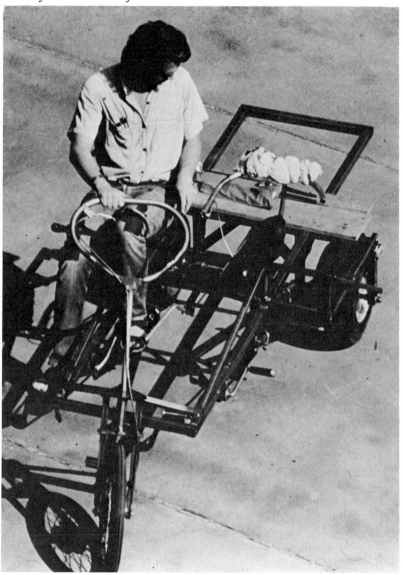

Figure 5-16. *Bath restraint for small or handicapped students. Designed by Mohammed Azali Bin Abdul Rahim, a postgraduate student of the author's at Manchester Polytechnic.*

The worst offenders are what the trade calls "combos." These are combinations of high chairs and toilet seats (imagine yourself as a grown-up, eating and urinating in the same chair!); car safety seats and strollers; and high chairs with clip-on activity trays. Most of these combos make no sense, and combinations that could really ease parents' and babys' lives are not made.

While carrying on research into infant needs, my students and I discovered a gap in the available product range. Every year a disturbingly large number of small children drown in only a few inches of water. Many, but by no means all, of these children are handicapped. A mother bathing her child in a basin, sink, or bathtub may be temporarily diverted by another child or a ringing phone. By neglecting to remove the wet baby from the tub, even a normal child might drown in only a foot of water. Mohammed Azali Bin Abdul Rahim, a postgraduate student from Malaysia developed a security bath restraint (figure 5-16). This blow-molded plastic back, equipped with secure safety strapping, keeps the child in an upright position and prevents drowning.

The device has proven itself useful for small children, and a virtual necessity for the smaller constituency of handicapped and retarded infants. Once again, the design stems directly from people. Design humanization has been achieved through a symbiotic relationship between parents, babies, and designers.

6
Decentralization

The task is not to construct ever-larger structures but to decompose the organizations that overwhelm us and to seek less abstract and remote dependencies.

SHELDON S. WOLIN

A S systems and institutions become more complex, there is a strong, universal desire to oppose the accelerating drive toward centralization. How else can you explain the fact that all of the candidates in the 1980 American presidential election (including five independent candidates) agreed on one thing—decentralization and a turning away from bigness. Over the last ten years, political figures as diverse as Mao Tse Tung, the Pope, and right-wing Central American generals have all emphasized the need for local autonomy, small systems, and decentralization.

In critical writings, and more specifically, in books for designers and architects, a parallel enthusiasm for decentralized structures has asserted itself. The *Whole Earth Catalogue*, my own *Design for the Real World* and Schumacher's *Small is Beautiful* paved the way in the early 1970s. Since then, Kirkpatrick Sale's *Human Scale*, Barbara Ward's *Progress for a Small Planet*, and Warren Johnson's *Muddling Toward Frugality* are just a few of the volumes that have advocated a basic rethinking and restructuring of the way we live.[1]

There are a number of reasons why people are striving for the small. To begin with, there is a deep-seated human need to deal with structures that can be understood and intellectually encompassed. We like to feel that we are in control. We enjoy thinking that we can, to some degree, control our actions and their consequences. These feelings are powerfully reinforced by the alarming growth of electronic information gathering and the mass media. In terms of information, entertainment, and news, the global village is in danger of becoming a global slum. Much of modern technology discourages independence, local autonomy, self-reliance, and decentralized modes of living. In *The Private Future*, Martin Pawley has painted an appalling view of this emerging ethnocentric future.[2]

A more optimistic view is possible. In a world that is both energy starved and resource poor, many technological inventions work best on a decentralized level. Solar power, windmills, methane digestion, building insulation, and many other things have not prospered, and may even have suffered because of this. The thinking and the technology are there but because both hardware and software work best when used on a personal level by individual households, the power companies are not interested.

For these reasons, the arguments against centralization are compelling in architecture, urban planning, and design. We can make a strong case for decentralization in terms of large systems and structures as well as in terms of human use and social accounting. Of course, smaller, more manageable structures are both productive and admirable. Schumacher and Sale pile argument upon argument until the very weight of their books become a powerful argument for reasonable size.

Despite what the gurus for decentralization and apologists for centralization might say, no simple choice is available. It is impossible only to favor centralization; it is equally absurd to be an apostle for decentralization. Although most of us have a strong bias toward decentralization, by itself it can never really work because we live in an interdependent society where government, law, and industrial processes are still highly centralized.

Instead, we must learn to resolve the seeming contradictions by considering the opposites holistically and simultaneously. The diagram (figure 6-1) of the monad or the *yin* and *yang* shows the relationship between two seemingly contradictory extremes. Let the black area stand for the concentrated; the apex of a pyramidal power structure; the large, controlled coalition; the unitary concentrated center. Let the white area stand for the dispersed, broad, unfocused, locally autonomous, many-headed decentralized process. The two movements coexist and fuse into one another to establish a perfect circle. Within the inky pool of central authority shines a bright torch of decentralization. In the white expanse of decentralization, a black area of amalgamation is visible.

We do need some centralization. Goods based on silicon chips, for example, need to be manufactured and assembled in "clean rooms," and are therefore most efficiently made in large factories.

Figure 6-1. *The yin-yang monad: a superb paradigm for looking at the world holistically.*

But in many ways, these chip-based products provide measures of independence for decentralized modes of living. Photovoltaic cells are another example. These are the most efficient way of converting solar power to energy. Presently they are fairly expensive—but only large centralized mass production facilities will bring down their price.

Despite the need for some centralization, designers should continue to seek solutions that can work on a local level. Industrial designers should introduce solutions that encourage design for human scale. Architects and city planners should not accept vast concentrated clusters as a given, but should work toward diversification and greater local choice.

The work of Frank Lloyd Wright can serve as an example. When asked to build a house, Wright, whenever possible, used only local materials. Many of his homes in the midwest used wood from abandoned local barns that had been painstakingly taken apart. This was no aesthetic whim. Lumber that has weathered thirty seasons in Minnesota will work well in the same location and climate. Sandstone or fieldstone that has survived Arizona summers will build perfect walls in the same area. Transplants do not work nearly as well.

Broadacre City was Wright's utopian plan to decentralize the entire United States.[3] Wright began working on the Broadacre City concept in the early 1930s, and continued until his death in 1959. Although it was never actually built, the individual homes, schools, and buildings that made up the master plan were built all over the country. Broadacre City's enchanting mix of rural and semirural neighborhoods, set in benign landscapes and linked by meandering paths and safe roads, was based on Jeffersonian ideals, and demonstrated Wright's attempt to transfer the values of his nineteenth century roots to the second half of the twentieth century. From 1949 to 1976 Broadacre City inspired China's planners to combine heavy industry, farms, universities, schools, hospitals, light industry, shops, cultural centers, and housing into one meaningful whole.

In industrial and product design, a number of questions are usually asked before work begins. One of these should be: are decentralized production and smaller manufacturing runs possible? From this, a second question arises. If smaller production runs and localized, decentralized production are possible, what are the benefits? Frequently, one of the main benefits is the possibility of producing tools and artifacts customized for local use or individual users. One example of how this can work has already been given in Chapter 5 with the bicycle-truck, the grain mill being worked on in many different countries, and other examples. A few more may substantiate the point.

In Chapter 2, do-it-yourself furniture designed for the residents of Wayne Miner and developed so that it could be easily built, was discussed. This is an excellent example of decentralization at work. By making the furniture inexpensive and easy to build, and by providing clear assembly instructions, the needs of the inhabitants of Wayne Miner were served. Not only could the residents choose between different pieces of furniture, but they could also select the color, texture, and decoration. Through their own work and through the individual choice of the special features, the pieces become personal and meaningful to each family. John Koester's muscle-powered truck mentioned in Chapter 5, serves as another example of decentralized design that is highly adaptive. Individual bicycle shops can fit each vehicle to the specific requirements of its users, and to the terrain on which it will be used.

In some cases, the need for decentralization becomes an overriding consideration. Design in a developing country helps to make us see this in its clearest form. There is a need for governments to communicate with their people. In many developing countries the tasks of communication and education are made difficult through the lack of a common language.

In Africa, official languages often reflect the colonial origins of a country. In Nigeria, for example, where the official language is English, thirty-three tribal languages, several Arab dialects and 218 local dialects are spoken. The majority of people living in the countryside are either illiterate, or speak only tribal dialects. Newspapers and books are usually printed in English, yet the people speak Kanuri.

In 1976, the governments of Nigeria and Tanzania asked me to develop a universal symbolic language to make it easier for them to communicate vital information to their people. This included information on subjects such as public health, diet, farming, and birth control. This work was done with the help of Mohammed Azali Bin Abdul Rahim and in consultation with people in the bush. However, research into sociocultural factors convinced the design team that this simplistic solution could not possibly work for the following reasons:

1. Anthropological studies had demonstrated that there were no universal symbols that were cross cultural. To develop a universal symbolic language and then teach it to an entire population would be more difficult than teaching conventional reading and writing skills.

2. To teach yet another language, a sort of graphic Esperanto, to preliterate people also implied freezing them in their preliterate state.[4]

3. In most developing countries, there is an oral story-telling tradition. Because of this, the ability to memorize is highly developed and prized, and the spoken word is more powerful than the written word.

4. Because there was no one predominant language, communication required decentralization according to linguistic groupings.

The design team's solution was to suggest a cassette-tape player that could be made (or at least assembled) in developing countries. This cassette player would be used to play educational tapes to the people in their own dialect.

Sophisticated cassette tape units are already used in developing countries, but are usually restricted to large cities and towns. In order to test our design concept, Philips cassette recorders were taken to rural areas in Africa where the people were encouraged to experiment with them. Although they learned to use them quickly, it soon became clear that certain modifications were necessary:

1. Although it was essential to use existing cassette-tape technology, the mechanics of the unit were greatly simplified. All unnecessary circuits, mechanisms, and controls (pause, record, and monitor) were eliminated.

2. Only two controls were provided: a volume knob (that communicated its function graphically) and a T-shaped on/off switch (which also controlled forward/reverse).

3. The battery case was externalized and held the two batteries in correctly aligned positions with no reference to positive and negative. The batteries were provided prepackaged so that they could only attach to the tape player in one way. The tape player consequently became smaller.

4. The housing for the unit was a three-part, plastic, injection-molded casing that would not be affected by tropical conditions. It was designed for manufacturing capabilities of developing countries. This housing (or shroud) is of great importance because tropical vermin are attracted by insulation wires and the chemicals on circuit boards. Humidity, dust, sand, and mud pose further problems. To make greater decentralized design participation by the people themselves possible, alternative housings were submitted for the people's consideration. The ingenuity of the people in developing countries will eventually result in far better designs.

The final prototype (figures 6-2, 6-3, and 6-4) was named Batta-Kōya, which means "talking teacher" in Hausa, and it received the Kyoto honors award at the 1981 ICSID/ICOGRADA/IFI Conference in Helsinki. Batta-Kōya is not an attempt to provide a special cassette tape unit for third world countries. Grundig, Philips, Sony, Panasonic, Hitachi, and Uher recorders are already available in the cities and towns of the developing world. This unit is a "talking teacher" for people in the African bush, the mountains and forests of South America, and the remote villages of New Guinea.

Some designers might say that taking an existing tape player and modifying its controls and battery case is simply styling. But using off-the-shelf hardware makes good sense in an energy deprived part of the world. Tools of this sort are by their very nature transnational, culture-preserving, and metapolitical. They increase understanding and learning on all levels by providing decentralized answers to decentralized needs.

Figure 6-2. *Batta-Kōya designed by the author and Mohammed Azali Bin Abdul Rahim together with indigenous people from Nigeria and Tanzania.*

Figure 6-3. *Alternative case for Batta-Kōya made of bamboo and calabash.*

Figure 6-4. *Alternative case for Batta-Kōya made of plaited and woven grasses.*

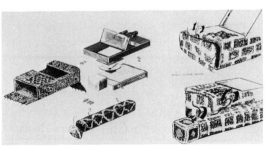

We have established the importance of decentralization, but an example may demonstrate how decentralization can help define objectives and bring about better design solutions.

During the last forty years, mass-produced housing has been widely discussed. Assembly line-produced automobiles and trailers have usually been used as examples of how it could work. Wartime prefabs were used some forty years ago, when Buckminster Fuller developed his prefabricated circular house for the Beechcraft Corporation in 1943. But the idea never really caught on. Today, with new insights into solar and other alternative energy sources, it is possible to develop a conceptual idea for such a home.

With the comfort of hindsight, we now realize how lucky we were to partially escape mass-produced housing. As automated assembly lines and computerized work stations proliferate in automobile production, consumers in many countries are demanding an increasing number of options in the cars they buy.

Even if we disregard the problems of the assembly line, the mass-produced car does not make much sense, when considering the macroenvironment in which the car will be used. We have seen leatherette dashboards buckle, crack, peel, deform, or melt on cars driven in the hot climates of the southwestern United States, Australia, and Southern Italy. Considering the fact that the cars were designed for climates like Detroit, Milan, Oxford, and Wolfsburg, this comes as no great surprise. We have also observed windshields shatter in the midwestern United States and northern Europe where the wind-chill factor can reach $-40°F$. In communities that border the desert (for example, Texas and Saudi Arabia), the drastic changes between day and nighttime temperatures have caused some early automatic, fuel-injection systems to go berserk.

In homes, the influences of the macroenvironment are even more important, one good reason why our conceptual house should not be designed for mass production. There are well-designed kit houses available right now. Some of the best of these are made in Norway. Wood, connectors, and other parts are bought as a unit, together with the plans. Most of these houses are intended as vacation homes or ski lodges. Having gazed with awe at an A-frame ski lodge designed to withstand a snow load of thirty-six inches serving as a beach hut in Fort Lauderdale, Florida, I feel that the design is not wholly appropriate. The very roof design that sheds snow in the north also keeps out sunlight in the south.

What is relevant for the design and building of such a home? The kit-house plans already in existence are in many cases well-crafted and logically designed. But other important questions should be considered:

1. *Climate.* Although the continental United States can be divided into seven climatic zones, there are more than three dozen microclimates. Degrees of insulation, wall thickness and roofing materials will differ from place to place. Just as the vestibule is absolutely essential in extremely cold climates, the thick wall structure of adobe-type housing is a must in the Southwest. Covered walkways are appropriate in areas subject to heavy rainstorms such as Florida, South Carolina, and Louisiana. The roof overhangs on the south side of a house needs to be computed exactly. The function of a roof overhang is simple—to shield rooms that face the south from the hot midday sun in the summer and yet permit warming rays to flood the room during the winter. Specifying the precise length of the overhang can be done on the back of an old envelope in five minutes, but it must be done for each separate locality. Positioning a house according to prevailing wind directions, the contours of the land, stands of trees, and watersheds will also differ from site to site.

2. *Size.* In Western Europe and even more so in North America, our homes have become warehouses for storing accumulated consumer goods. Our preoccupation with making things bigger and better has resulted in our homes expanding more and more. Originally, the vast space was a luxury, but we can no longer afford to heat and cool large meandering structures. It has been estimated that at any given moment there is at least one spare "guest room" in every three American homes which, though fully furnished and heated, is used only two to three weeks a year. This is just one example of energy waste. In general, as soon as we inhabit our large homes we immediately start shopping for furniture,

furnishings, and knickknacks to help bring the vast spaces down to size. True luxury is the ability to do without. Mies van der Rohe's "less is more" sounds less paradoxical when restated as "less is necessary," but it is more honest.

3. *Energy sources.* The precise width of roof overhangs and the varying needs for insulation have been discussed. This is only the beginning. The use of greenhouse walls, passive or active solar collectors, photovoltaic cells, and wind generators are just some of the choices that each homeowner can make. The use of a Clivus Multrum (a toilet that successfully composts organic wastes without water, chemicals or electricity), is one more device that could become a plug-in/plug-out component in individually developed homes. Methane digesters and closed-system micro-ecological plant and fish farms (similar to the prototypes developed by the New Alchemy Institute) could also be added to this list.

4. *Materials.* Earlier in this chapter I described how Frank Lloyd Wright cannibalized existing barns to find well-weathered wood, which he would then use in his houses in the same area. Fieldstone, brick, limestone, and even adobe components, work best in the locality they come from. Fiscally, this makes sense. It costs a great deal to transport building materials. Add to this the energy bills for transport, and the result is even more skewed. Functionally and aesthetically, local materials work best.

5. *The design.* Considering what has been written so far, we can see how the house design develops. It is not a design, but rather a scrapbook of design possibilities. It begins with a basic house kit, adjusted to reduce room sizes and to allow for the incorporation of energy-saving and energy-generating systems. The designs vary according to the specific microenvironment in which each home will stand, providing low, broad, sweeping roof overhangs on the north, shorter ones on the south. There are vestibules, covered paths, or taller rooms with ceiling fans, depending on the climate. Each of these house kits differs in the size, number of people accommodated, and materials used. When wood is needed that will absorb moisture easily, it would be impractical to cart cypress to California or redwood to Florida. Both woods do the same job, and they do it best in their own locale.

What we have designed is something like a *Whole Earth Catalogue* of owner-built or owner-contracted homes. The degrees to which the design is successful depends on decentralization. But the monad, the yin and yang of centralization and decentralization, still holds. What has been centralized in the above system is data and information. The rest is open to autonomy and innovation.

7
Suffer Little Children: Design Education

What do we believe in—or, if you are made that way, what does God want? Quality or quantity? You can either believe in a world teeming with poor, underfed, uneducated and brute-like billions of unhealthy human beings, or you can believe that the human race should comprise a smaller number of higher quality people living fuller and more richly-colored lives. Everyone faced with this question will elect the second alternative, even though many religions try to make it impossible to pursue it. But to achieve the second goal is almost unbelievably difficult, for it involves an attempt to quantify the virtually unquantifiable.

PHILIP WILLS[1]

ONE place where design can be of great help is in education. Not just with the education of designers, but with the education of everyone—specifically children from kindergarten and nursery school all the way through secondary education and beyond.

Design can help in four ways. First, there is the traditional role—educating students in design at universities, polytechnics and technical institutes. Second, there is the education of young children and teenagers, a new and vital area. Third, is the physical structure of schools (from both an architectural and environmental viewpoint) that is, and will continue to be, the proper concern of architects and environmental designers. School curricula and teaching methods can be greatly aided by systems design. Finally, there is educational software—seats, desks, tables, teaching aids, wall charts, teaching machines, and audiovisual materials—in desperate need of creative innovation and redesign.

In *Design for the Real World* I wrote: "Design is the most powerful tool in the hands of mankind with which man can shape his environment and, by extension, eventually himself." In the final analysis, man shapes society and his future by what is taught to the young, how it is taught and why. Design education should be introduced into preprimary, primary, and secondary schools, instead of limiting it to vocational and occupational studies at a post-secondary level. It could easily take the place of the art education and art appreciation courses now being taught.

Although many strides have already been made in this direction, primarily in places such as England, this view will undoubtedly be attacked as philistine. But instead of viewing this as an attack on the arts, examine the positive results that can come from design education. Design is a conscious and intuitive effort to impose meaningful order. This need lies at the base of all meaningful art. In addition, it is one of the most basic human drives (both intellectual and emotional)—to order, arrange, organize, and discipline a seemingly chaotic environment. This statement is based on twenty-five years of design experience and half a century of living experience. The search for good form clarifies a latent sense of harmony and order in most people. To bring order out of chaos is a deep-rooted desire in all people with a sane view of the world. Design is both the underlying matrix of order and the tool that creates it.

Enough polemics. There are examples and case histories that will aid this argument. Most generalizations can mislead. Nonetheless looking at entire populations, it can be argued that expectations for elegant and simple design are not as widely shared in some countries as in Denmark and Finland. Having lived and worked in the Scandinavian countries and elsewhere, I have come to the conclusion that the main difference lies in design education.

In Denmark, design education forms an important part of day-to-day lessons in kindergarten and nursery school. This is also true in Finland. Compare the restrained and pure tile designs brought home by kindergarten children in Copenhagen to the mawkish puppets made of used orange juice containers, tinsel, and mint wrappers in England, or the Thanksgiving turkeys made of pie plates and cotton wool in the United States with the simple and austere cutting boards made by children of the same age in Finland. Little can justify the cultural phenomenon known as art education. The British and American students have taken rubbish, turned it into ornamental rubbish, and then been told that they have created art. Do not misunderstand. We need art. Painting, poetry, music, dance, and sculpture give us great joy. In addition, recent psychological studies have shown clearly that babies and small children exposed to music and painting develop perceptual skills far more quickly than those children who are not.

We are all involved in design. As end users we are both consumers and victims of the environment, buildings, tools, and artifacts that make up our world. If, as stated above, design is a conscious and intuitive effort to impose meaningful order, then the how and why of this should be taught.

For many years I have felt that what is routinely taught as "foundations design" and "basic design" in Western Europe and North America is taught to the wrong people at the wrong time. These courses are generally taught at post-secondary design and architectural schools to young people between the ages of seventeen and twenty-one. The projects in these courses offer splendid opportunities for discovery and self-knowledge. Such basic exercises as supporting a standard brick 16 inches above a table top with the least number of toothpicks forming a tower; designing and making a spinning top that will continue to spin for four or five minutes; arranging squares of textured material according to roughness and smoothness; packaging an uncooked egg in such a way that it can be dropped six feet without damage; making visual comparisons between ships, boats, and submarines on the one hand, and fish and dolphins on the other; comparing seagulls, hummingbirds, bats, and insects with helicopters, ornicopters, aircraft and gliders—these and many other basic design exercises are splendid nudges to the imagination. But they are wasted on eighteen-year-old design students. These same exercises could be taught to six-year-olds, when basic design studies should begin.

I have taught standard university-level design courses to six- and seven-year-olds—the results have in many cases exceeded my expectations for university students.

Examining what makes a teacup work, why a certain chair is uncomfortable, why one screwdriver raises blisters while another does not, what is good quality and what is not, why some cars are safe and comfortable while others are "unsafe at any speed," what makes one room soothing and another distressing—all this can be explored in secondary schools. One of these secondary schools at Bramhall in Cheshire, England invited me to work with their twelve- and thirteen-year-olds on a major design exercise—to look at a product, evaluate and criticize it, then design and build a better version. Their solutions were amazingly apt, as good or better than solutions that might have been produced at a polytechnic or art-college level. One of the finest courses in industrial design in the world is taught to fifteen- and sixteen-year-olds at a secondary school in Belgrade, Yugoslavia.

While teaching design to young men and women in Denmark, I was often frightened at the thought of their entry into the profession during a deepening economic depression. Many of these young people ended up filling beer bottles at Carlsburg or driving taxis around Copenhagen, but it was amazing how their design training helped them while they carried out these temporary jobs. For one thing, it raised their public conscience, for another it increased their insistence on quality. Even when working on a bottling line in a brewery, they questioned how things worked, often suggesting simple alterations, which improved productivity and the quality of the work environment. Because they had been taught to evaluate, they did not accept work procedures unquestioned. At the brewery, for instance, a student pointed out to management that they did not have to wear uncomfortable earphones, the machines could be soundproofed instead. The students' design education carried over into their home life as well. They took greater care in buying things to furnish their homes, in selecting the tools they used, and in choosing the homes

123

themselves. They noticed and commented on the quality of public spaces, street furniture, and anything else that increased the sense of a cohesive community.

The physical structure of schools, classroom environments, and the conceptual structuring of schools are all important issues. They are being explored by architects, environmental designers, and systems designers in many parts of the world. What is needed is more direct feedback from users—school children, teachers, and administrators.

Children are naturally active. If they are to be kept in classrooms for many hours a day with limited exercise periods, the classrooms should at least be visually exciting. Today classrooms compete with discos, amusement parks, video arcades, and other stimulating public spaces for children's attention. In addition, depending upon the home the child comes from, the classroom may be the most exciting place the child visits all day. Dull classrooms represent a kind of sensory deprivation not conducive to learning.

One critical issue is the nearly total lack of horizontal crossover information from school to school on a worldwide basis. What is called for is an information network that will encourage success and prevent obvious mistakes from being repeated.

Finally, there is the software used in schools. A few examples from recent practice will demonstrate how and where design can have its greatest impact in this area. In 1981, one of my classes was asked to consider the problems of educating young children. The ensuing discussions lasted for several weeks. To reestablish some link with the real world, the students were asked to visit schools, talk to teachers, and play with school children and interview them. The students were shocked by what they learned. With only a few exceptions, the teachers they spoke to could be divided into two groups—the old and tired who had long since given up and the young and tired who were just on the point of giving up. Both groups seemed bereft of new ideas and were unwilling to give new approaches a chance. The students seemed to be suffering from the same depression. They considered going to school an unpleasant chore that had to be faced. Principals and school superintendents were either bureaucratic robots, incapable idealists or brutish disciplinarians.

As for the teaching aids, there were many educational toys, teaching machines, and language learning laboratories that did a superb job. But many other teaching aids had become highly commercialized. Classroom teachers and administrators had a difficult choice, selecting from catalogs bursting with meaningless puzzles, moronic mathematical quizzes, and trashy plastic learning toys carefully developed to trivialize the act of learning. A typical catalog was twice the size of the Manhattan telephone book and all of the items listed are extraordinarily expensive.

Meeting and playing with children and spending all night in discussion with those teachers who still dared to care, a new reality emerged. It was possible to design simple things on a small scale that would improve the quality of learning and participation on many levels.

The design group found no panacea that would radically change the structure of schools. That change must (and will inevitably) come directly from children, parents, and committed classroom teachers. Instead, a few small gadgets were presented.

Many children dread mathematics. The concepts of addition, multiplication, and fractions and that two halves make a whole are extraordinarily difficult to teach in primary school. How to find the area of an equilateral triangle or a parallelogram, the Pythagorean theorem and many other mathematical complexities are difficult for children to grasp. Lectures and demonstrations can be boring and textbooks are either remote or make dismal attempts at humor. Only the introduction of computers has brought about new teaching methods and made finding out about mathematics and geometry a challenge for many children. But computers cost money and are still unavailable to many school systems.

One of my students designed a combination toy and game with which children might learn mathematics by their sense of touch through their fingertips. The Chinese saying, "I look and I see; I listen and I hear; I do and I understand," is given new meaning when children learn about numbers through hands-on experience.

Floppy Math (figure 7-1), like so many brilliant ideas, is dis-

Figure 7-1. *"Floppy Math": A learning game designed by Holly Hughes as a student at the Kansas City Art Institute, demonstrating the 4 × ¼ = 1.* (Photograph by Paul Wise)

mayingly simple. A comparison square, sixteen inches square (and subdivided into a grid of four times four squares), an activity square (the same size as the comparison square), several smaller squares and a number of right-angled triangles in various sizes constituted one set. All the squares were bright cotton, printed in contrasting colors on each side. The comparison square was also double sided, with a contrasting grid of sixteen squares on each surface.

The comparison square was never handled—it was there to count off quarters, eighths, and sixteenths. A number of games were possible with the activity square. It could be folded diagonally or vertically to demonstrate the areas of triangles or, by merely counting the layers of fabric, that two halves make one. Fold it once more, and four quarters make a whole, and so on. By selecting a right-angled triangle and making squares consisting of two triangles each along both base edges and the hypotenuse (figure 7-2), the theorem $a^2 + b^2 = c^2$ could be shown.

Many other manipulations are possible. What makes the solution

126

Figure 7-2. *The "Floppy Math" kit demonstrating the Pythagorean Theorem. (Photograph by John Charlton)*

truly elegant, however, is the fact that it is a truly open-ended game. What can be done with the squares and triangles is only limited by the imagination of the children and teachers. The possibilities are endless. In addition, these same squares and triangles can be used to explore topological transformations, space warps, and harmonic theory by more advanced students.

The outlay for materials is minimal, and the different game boards can be sewn by children or their parents. Decentralized design and entrepreneurial manufacturing can make the game available to schools everywhere. Because of the low cost of materials and minimal equipment needed (a sewing machine), small manufacturers and even cottage or village level groups could make such a product.

About twenty years ago, when work with computers was a more laborious process than today, I saw my engineering design students struggling with the task of generating random numbers. Random numbers, as used in the computer sciences, are two sets of three random digits from zero to nine. Since it is psychologically impossible for anyone to generate numbers that are truly random, students and people working with computers had to buy books consisting entirely of thousands of listings of random numbers. The job of proofreading and printing these volumes made them expensive and in addition they were tedious to use. Trying to develop a simpler, less expensive, and more pleasant way to generate such numbers, I designed icosahedral dice (figure 7-3).

Since normal gaming dice generate a limited set of random numbers (from one to six) I experimented with a series of ten-sided geometric constructions (deltahedra) that would accommodate ten digits. Because they would not roll easily, a survey was made of all polyhedra (the five Platonic solids: cube, tetrahedron, octahedron, dodecahedron, and icosahedron) as well as the seventeen semiregular Archimedean solids and their duals. It was plain that no easy rolling ten-sided solid could be developed that was not also geometrically loaded.

The icosahedron, with twenty equilateral faces, was the most

Figure 7-3.
Icosahedral dice used for generating random numbers for computer programmers. Author's design.

spherelike, rolled easily, and permitted the digits zero to nine to be displayed twice on each die. Two rolls of three dice (their digital order was color coded so that red meant the first digit in a three digit number, yellow the second and blue the third) would give a six-digit random number. The set was marketed for under $6.00 (one tenth the price of the book).

Two students used my concept of icosahedral dice for a whole series of learning games. Their wooden dice are about the size of a small apple and are made of walnut or birch. They feel pleasant, roll easily, and are extraordinarily good looking (figures 7-4 and 7-5).

Each of the twenty faces of these icosahedral dice bears a word, number, concept, or color. Two or more dice are needed for a game. Dice sets have been made for teaching geography, mathematics, number theory, sentence structure, plot development, history, biology, and other subjects. In a typical geography game, three dice are rolled. The three resulting die faces show a country, a political, economic, or social feature and a time scale. A roll might yield:

> Brazil
> natural resources
> in 10 years

Taking the three in combination might prompt a classroom discussion.

In another game six dice (three from geography and three from biology) were combined resulting in:

> Buffalo
> habitat
> predator
> USA
> 200 years ago
> food supply

Three dice with twenty faces each can result in 8,000 possible combinations. From time to time the dice may produce silly

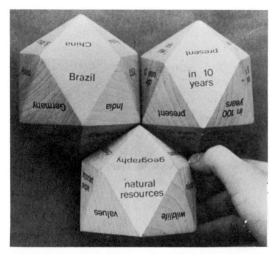

Figure 7-4. *A set of the large icosahedral dice being used in a geography exercise by nine-year-old students. Designed by Bernie Rosen and Becky Wilson, as students at the Kansas City Art Institute. (Photograph by John Charlton)*

Figure 7-5. *Nine learning dice by Rosen and Wilson. (Photograph by Paul Wise)*

combinations, such as:

USA
manufacturing
2,000 years ago

But no harm is done. Everyone can have a good laugh and an interesting discussion may even result from the nonsense throw. The dice have endless applications.

It has also been suggested that the dice could also be used as a psychological testing tool in such diverse areas as Family Profile Preference (FPP) and Thematic Aperception Tests (TAT).

I have now taken these icosa-dice a step further. Using a method I developed in the early 1960s for creative problem-solving called "bisociation technique,"[2] I have used the tetrahedral dice to expand this technique to what I have labeled "trisociation." Instead of bringing the idea of a product to be designed into random collision with one of seven stimulus words (resulting in seven different free association solutions), in trisociation, played with seven dice, 1,280,000,000 solutions are possible. Even in a trisociation game using only four dice, there are 64,000 possible choices.

The system is elegant, because it performs a type of solution seeking that even computers are incapable of. Until the intellectual heirs of Fritz von Foerster develop a random hunting circuit, the icosahedral dice are the only simple, effective way of doing the job.

Most children between the ages of five and twelve are healthy, physically active bundles of stored energy. Schools seem like prisons to many of them. Their purely physical need for movement and exercise is often so frustrated that their attention wanders and their inborn need to acquire knowledge, their aggressive curiosity is stifled and sidetracked. Packed into dull schoolrooms, forced to sit on whatever cheap and uncomfortable chair came in at the lowest bid to the school board, they fidget, squirm, and spend most of their time trying to think up yet another way of crossing their legs.

A student of mine decided to explore a multipositional seating unit. He investigated a classroom perch (figure 7–6) designed nearly eleven years ago by Steven Lynch, a student of mine at Purdue University. Another unit, designed in Denmark and Norway, was also intensively studied. The goal was to design a chair that was ergonomically outstanding and that could be built at home or at school. The student argued correctly that his unit (figure 7-7), unlike Steven Lynch's, should be a substitute for regular classroom chairs, instead of acting as additional pieces of furniture. His seat has six different main positions. Three of these positions are semikneeling (figure 7-8). Three more offer

Figure 7-6. *Alternative seating designed by Oddvin Rykken and Hans Christian Mengshoel of Norway.* (*Photograph courtesy of Hag A/S, Oslo, Norway*)

conventional sitting, reclining, or lounging positions. The unit has been tested and permits restless children to change from upright seating to a sort of controlled sprawl.

The unit is small. A plywood base and backplate are covered with layers of high-density Styrofoam plastic and medium-density polyurethane. The cover is easily cleanable linen canvas. It is simple and chunky looking. Children have called it neat, cuddly,

Figure 7-7. *Alternative seating for do-it-yourself construction, designed by Robert Curtis Wilson as a student at the Kansas City Art Institute. Note the oval back rest, which also pushes against the child's stomach in some positions. This is important for some spastic and cerebral palsy children.*

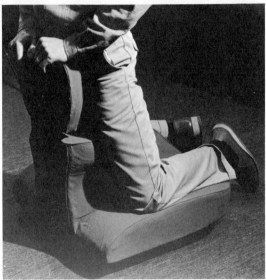

Figure 7-8. *One of the positions possible with the multiuse classroom perch by Wilson.*

and cute. From an anthropomorphic viewpoint it helps establish good posture through continuous change.

The continuing assault on a child's sensibilities by beguiling advertisements—the frequently decerebrating program served up to children on television, the underlying capitalistic concept of "you are what you buy" and that you express yourself through objects—has made the task of education more difficult. But as we have seen in many other areas, committed designers working closely with children, parents, and teachers can help to turn things round.

8
Design for Human Scale: Design Ecology

Think globally,
act locally,
plan modestly.

RENÉ DUBOS AND VICTOR PAPANEK[1]

IEWING design, we can recognize the importance of ecology. More importantly, we can see that design and ecology are strongly linked. There is a relationship between the way designers and ecologists see the world. It is impossible to design the simplest artifact, the most basic machine or the humblest shelter without seeing the world as a whole. Some might say this attitude is idealistic and impractical, but considering the mess practical thinking has gotten us into, I believe idealism is needed now more than ever.

135

Many of the environmental problems facing mankind today are the results of mistaken human choices, the products of bad design. For nearly 2,000 years we have tried to shape the world to our will, but as Thomas Mann had Felix Krull observe in *Confessions of Felix Krull, Confidence Man*, "He who really loves the world shapes himself to please it."

Konrad Lorenz said, "Man is by nature a creature of culture," implying that civilized human culture has become an integral part of the biological evolution of our species. Human culture is potentially the most quickly adaptable of our features, providing we can intelligently decide which way to go. Our culture, and the changes in our culture, are helped along by design and ecology and consequently influence ecology and design. The basic truth at the heart of ecology is that nature is indivisible, and cannot therefore be comprehended through the study of its isolated fragments. Ecologists are interdisciplinary students of nature because they have discovered that nature is itself interdisciplinary. A biologist can photograph, describe, and taxonomically classify a whale, for example. But the ecologist must understand the chemistry of oceans in order to study whale behavior. He needs to know about the whale's dietary needs, and about the use of ambergris for perfume and whale bone for girdles. The psychology and market economics of whale hunters are as much a part of the ecology of whales as the hydrothermal currents that influence their migratory patterns. Specialists will claim that detailed knowledge of such diverse subjects is impossible. Ecologists will readily agree, but will point out that whales cannot be truly understood unless all of this varied information is somehow related.

Design is to technology what ecology is to biology. Specialists will again insist that subjects such as anthropology, philosophy, engineering, the arts, biology, and psychology—all relevant to design—require highly disciplined intellectual skills and therefore cannot be mastered together with the equally complex disciplines of architecture and design. Designers will not claim that it is possible to acquire all of the expertise needed for a full understanding of a difficult subject, but will maintain that design must take into account the subtle relationships between disciplines.

If the whole world could be shown broken down into little boxes like a table of organization, designers and ecologists would study the flow lines that connect the little boxes, while most other disciplines would peer myopically into each separate box. In addition, designers seek to discover new lines that were previously invisible to the specialists.

Both design and ecology are models invented by humans. No matter that all natural organisms are deeply involved in their own ecosystems—only we can describe how such systems work. The mental ability that allows us to change ecosystems (often causing their destruction) also helps us to create better systems. Our imagination gives us the power to create new ecosystems, destroy old ones, and explain existing ones. A relationship exists between design and ecology that may help to bring together intellect and intuition, science and art, and possibly even humans and nature. Aesthetics, the perception of beauty, is deeply rooted in natural forms and biological processes that exist with or without our perception. Our whole aesthetic value system is no more than abstract formulations of the natural as it exists within and around us. We find beauty in design only when it is compatible with forms and processes in nature.

There are deep-seated reasons for this. This relationship between design, esthetics, and biology demands greater understanding. H. J. Eysenck writes about his theory, based on experimentation, ". . . there exists some property of the nervous system which determines aesthetic judgments, a property which is biologically derived. . ."[2]

Let us examine the emotion brought about by the interaction between an object of beauty and an observer—the aesthetic reaction. If Eysenck's working hypothesis is correct (and every day more contributing data from the fields of genetics, botany, structural morphology, crystallography, and the arts seems to confirm it), then the aesthetic experience is a levitation from the unconscious to the conscious mind of complex memories that are triggered by "associational values" essential to the visual or aural contemplation of a beautiful object.[3] These hidden associational memories derive from the immemorial terrestrial environment of humans. It must be emphasized that these associations are hidden memory values, making investigation difficult. My meaning may be made clear if we look at some examples that have been familiar to humans and other animals for millions of years.

Color contrasts. We share our pleasure in color with many other animals. Describing the bower building activity of the bower birds of New Guinea and Australia, Dr. W. H. Thorpe writes, "They build bowers for courtship with brightly-coloured fruits or flowers which are not eaten but left for display and replaced when they wither . . . They stick to a particular colour scheme. Thus, a bird using blue flowers will throw away a yellow flower inserted by an experimenter, while a bird using yellow flowers will not tolerate a blue one."[4] Thorpe goes on to quote Robert Bridges, " '. . . it may well be that a sense of beauty came to those primitive bipeds earlier than to man.' " We have possessed an appreciation of color for millions of years. We tend to find delight when we look at flowers, rainbows, sunsets, snowflakes, and sea shells. Doing so arouses an aesthetic response in our conscious mind.

Shape. Quite aside from the dazzling color display, the gentle curve of a rainbow can, through associational values, release impressions stored in the collective unconscious based on an appreciation of the ever-present phenomenon of the earth's gravity—the lovely parabolic flight of a tossed stone, for example. The same unique form is shared by all parabolas, and the towering arc of the rainbow recalls these.

Proportion. Our appreciation of "good" proportion is based on our own body ratios. All over the world (with the exception of three or four pygmy tribes in Latin America and Africa), human proportions, regardless of body size, are nearly the same. The relationship of head size to body height, hand to forearm, forearm to arm, foot to thigh are, regardless of length, nearly identical in adults. It is this aspect of proportional empathy (or biological *Einfühlung*) that makes us respond positively to art from other cultures and the earliest relics of our past. With an educated eye we can find beauty, catharsis, or meaning in such disparate objects as the 30,000-year-old Willendorf Venus, the cave paintings of Lascaux and Altamira, an Eskimo shaman's mask, a Bombara fetish stick from Central Africa, Giotto's frozen angels, a Japanese

Emakimono painting, and a Sepik River mask from New Guinea. The significance is that while our capacity for aesthetic pleasure, related as it is to our bodily proportions, opens nearly all artistic productions to us, some of us may have trouble deriving pleasure from the art of pygmies. As a corollary to this, some pygmies and dwarves may find the aesthetic values of different proportioned people difficult to fathom.

Eidetic image. Tied closely to our deeply felt relationship with human proportion is the faint eidetic image of our personel selves. For instance, nowadays it is considered fashionable to be slim. Plump people are considered somewhat unsightly in western Europe, North and South America, and the Far East. Maybe this is why the women painted by Rubens, Titian and Renoir are less popular than they once were, and why, for this matter, the "fat" refrigerators, cookers, and household appliances of the 1920s seem so unattractive. It may also be the reason we now treasure the images of Modigliani and Giacometti, "slimline" refrigerators and "trimline" telephones.

Other proportions. Our collective unconscious allows us to positively respond to other proportional imprints. The chambered nautilus (*nautilus pompilius*) in figure 8-1 follows an exact logarithmic spiral. Other spiral curves can be found in sea shells and snails from the prehistoric ammonites (figure 8-2) to the murexes, including the precious wentletrap (figure 8-3), the spindle tibia (figure 8–4), and the Atlantic Sundial (figure 8-5). The spirally convoluted horns of animals such as the ibex, Barbary sheep, elands, Sardinian mouflon and the situtunga have been charted and described by T. A. Cook in *The Curves of Life* (London: Constable & Co., 1940).

Fibonacci. The Fibonacci series, which can be seen in the growth pattern of flowers and plants and as an "ideal" proportion in pine cones (figure 8-6), pineapples (figure 8-7), most cacti, and at the center of sunflowers, is another harmonic spiral organization that shapes our aesthetic perception. This spiral can assume a helical shape, which influences our thinking about divine proportion and led to the development of the Golden Section and Ideal Proportioning. Scientists are also motivated by this research for good form, and it is interesting to reread Watson's search for the

Figure 8-1. *Chambered nautilus* (nautilus pompilius L.).
(Photograph by John Charlton)

Figure 8-2. *Fossil ammonite.*
(Photograph by John Charlton)

Figure 8-3. *Precious wentletrap* (epitonium scalare L.) *Author's collection.* *(Photograph by John Charlton)*

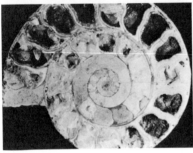

Figure 8-4. *Spindle tibia* (tibia fusus L.*) Author's collection. *(Photograph by John Charlton)*

Figure 8-5. *Atlantic sundial* (architechtonica nobilis R.*)* *(Photograph by John Charlton)*

Figure 8-6. *Base of pinecone.* *(Photograph by John Charlton)*

Figure 8-7. *Pineapple showing spiral configuration. (Photograph by John Charlton)*

141

helical DNA structure in this context. Dirac has gone so far as to state, "It is more important to have beauty in one's equations than to have them fit the experiment."[5]

Other organic patterns. The list of things which prompt an aesthetic response from our collective unconscious is infinite. There is the radial symmetry of a flower blossom or a snowflake which has given rise to many of the decorative patterns in Islamic architecture. In figures 8-8, 8-9, and 8-10, *radiolaria* (tiny marine organisms first classified by Haeckel over a hundred years ago) exhibit a geodesic spherical symmetry, which inspired Buckminster Fuller's geodesic dome. The multiaxial symmetric organization of crystals has had a powerful influence on much of the best recent architecture, from Bruce Goff's crystalline churches to John Lloyd Wright's Wayfarer's Chapel cantilevered out over the Pacific Ocean and Steve Baer's Zomes. All polyhedral geometry is derived from crystals. Baer's Zomes have "stretched" polyhedra, and provided the basis for the domes made of recycled automobile tops at Drop City, Colorado. In Great Britain, the best known example of crystal-based architecture is James Stirling's Cambridge University Mathematics building.[6] For centuries artists, designers, architects, and their followers have found aesthetic excitement in the shape of a woman's breast, the fold-over curve of rose petals and Easter lilies, the sensuous S-curve of a swan's neck. These seemingly different shapes are all based on a second-order curve, and for this reason we find the same excitement in the series of shells that make up the Sydney Opera House, the TWA terminal at Kennedy Airport in New York and the mosques and minarets of Islamic countries.

Psychology of perception and Gestalt. All human beings have a natural appreciation of pleasing shapes and forms. This appreciation of good form has a biological base. It is a psychophysiological function of the brain's search for order. From experiments with laboratory animals such as Karl Von Frisch's experiments with the dance of bees as a communications device and Konrad Lorenz's work with graylag geese and sticklebacks, we may safely assume that this search for order is present even in the lower species. The work of early Gestalt psychologists such as Wolfgang Köhler and Karl Koffka point to a strong biological basis for our experience of form, especially when taken in conjunction with some of the

Figure 8-8. *Marine organisms. (after Haeckel)*

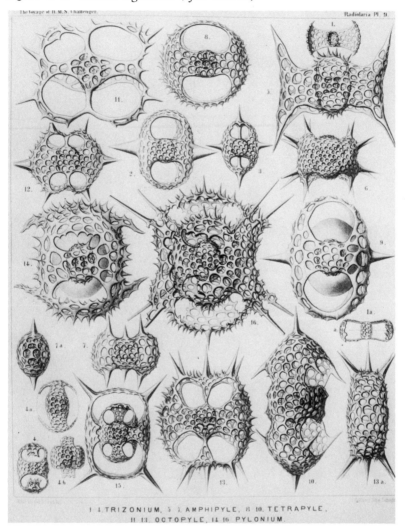

more courageous hypotheses of Wilhelm Reich. This instinct influences the way we design and make things as well as the way we relate to handsome objects. (See Katz, Ellis, and Rawlins in the Bibliography).

Cute. This sloppy, slang word has recently been used by bi-

Figure 8-9. *Marine organisms. (after Haeckel)*

I OROSPHAERA. 2-4 CONOSPHAERA. 5,6 ETHMOSPHAERA.
7-11 CERIOSPHAERA.

ologists, ethologists, and sociobiologists to describe the rather puzzling phenomenon that occurs when we are faced with a baby animal. "There is . . . an inborn response to characteristics of infants perceived as "cute," characteristics such as large eyes low in a head somewhat out of proportion, at least out of the adult

Figure 8-10. *Marine organisms. (after Haeckel)*

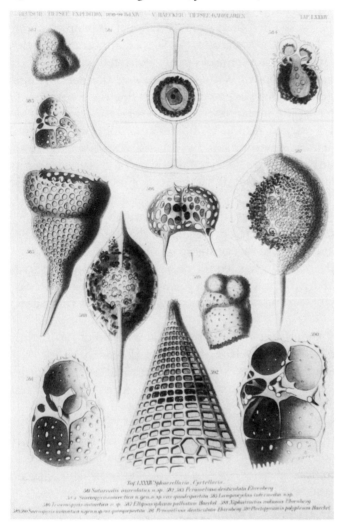

proportion, to the rest of the body, a set of characteristics shared by most mammalian young."[7] Since human beings are not the only animals that respond favorably—and protectively—to such features, some species have actually profited from this reaction. Such responses to infants occur in men as well as women. This "cute response" also works across species. Domestic animals such as dogs and cats often treat babies and young children with great tenderness. A duck-billed platypus is unfamiliar to people outside of Australia. Lacking any clue to the size or appearance of this odd animal, strangers nevertheless can usually tell when they are shown a young platypus. Without examining the species-preservation mechanisms involved here, it is plain that the cute response also helps to shape our nature-based view of aesthetics.

Culture is a learned response. There is no doubt that cultural responses, that is, environmentally learned responses, make us react differently to works of art, buildings, or designed objects from different cultures. But at the basis of it all lies the fact that began our argument—we find beauty in design only when it is compatible with forms and processes in nature.

Human beings must learn more about what the world is really like and spend less time dreaming about the kind of world they would like it to be if they could only change it. Both ecology and design deal with processes and relationships in the real world. In both lies the promise of reconnecting the isolated fragments.

We now move from the philosophical viewpoint of Arthur Koestler's "trivial plane"—from the big to the small.

Specialization in designed products can lead to greater dependency by the user. Compare the Model A or Model T Ford of half a century ago to today's cars equipped with automatic transmission, power steering, and power brakes. The early models were designed to be repaired and maintained by the owner or, if that was not possible, by the neighborhood garage. Today, so much can go wrong with sophisticated electronic and electric systems, automatic-fuel injections and power-window assists, that the owner is helpless in the face of mechanical failure. Maintenance, diagnosis, replacement, and repair depend on even more sophisticated electronic instruments, which the neighborhood mechanic can neither understand nor afford. Now compare today's cars with those we can expect by the mid-1980s. Dozens of microprocessors, computerized trip meters, and other chip-based ephemera make work on the car impossible for the owner.

Compare an office building of the 1880s with one designed and built a hundred years later. In its simplest form, a building consists of a skeleton (support, roof, and foundation), skin (walls, floors, and windows) and a circulatory system (heating, air conditioning, lighting, water access, and electric outlets). The skin and bones of yesterday's high-rise buildings were designed to insulate interior spaces, ventilate rooms through open windows, and perform the building's primary function—enclosing usable space superbly, efficiently, and for a long time. The structure and skin of the building used to represent the largest part of capital investment; the circulatory system was frequently incidental.

In today's office buildings the mechanical and electrical service systems represent the greatest outlay in capital and labor. These complex and sophisticated systems frequently need repair or replacement, but gaining access to them often involves the destruction of the fabric of the building. Many of the lighting, heating, and air conditioning systems of 1981 will become obsolete within ten to fifteen years, leading to the razing of structures to build new ones which will include the latest in systems design. There are, of course, brilliant exceptions to this, Mies van der Rohe's Illinois Institute of Technology, the Yale library by Skidmore, Owings, and Merrill, and James Stirling's Mathematics building at Cambridge being a few prominent examples.

Often the confrontation between a building and its subsidiary service functions can result in pathetically dystopian designs. Lae in northern Papua New Guinea is a university town close enough to the equator to lie enveloped in a circumambient haze of humidity and heat. University classroom buildings are low, two-story structures with ceilings high enough to keep rooms cool. Two opposing walls consist entirely of slit windows that direct prevailing winds through the rooms. Air circulation is assisted by large ceiling fans.

In the center of the campus, the architecture and engineering buildings rise a full twenty-one stories. All windows are fixed and there are no ceiling fans. The entire building has been designed around a central air conditioning system that is both inadequate to do the job and has only worked for nine days during the last four years. Designers, architects, and engineers sweating at their desks are getting a practical lesson in the dangers of inappropriate technology and the advantages of returning to simpler concepts. This is not a plea to return to the past. It is, however, a plea to

147

consider the past and the lessons it holds for us. Raiding the past for solutions demands wisdom and selectivity, but the rewards are substantial.

For the last twenty to thirty years, many young designers from the world's most highly developed countries have gone to practice in developing countries to help the underprivileged of the third world. Although they have gone to these countries as "experts," to help and teach, they have returned having learned a great deal about the fragile balance between man and nature.

Recycling materials and preserving things for as long as possible are simply not issues in many developing countries. In much of the southern hemisphere, ecological understanding and innovation are forced upon people by poverty. With an average annual income of $150 to $1000, the multiple use of tools is a necessity. Throwaway cigarette lighters are carefully refilled and repaired and automobiles are driven for up to fifty years. In Africa and elsewhere, almost all throwaway goods are valued (see, for example, figure 8-11). Wine bottles, jam jars, and even glass splinters (used in local glassblowing establishments) are collected.

Automobile tires and tire cases are one of the most dangerous bits of trash in western society. They are virtually indestructible, surviving in trash dumps forever, and creating toxic fumes when burned. In developing countries, tires are used until they have a mirror-smooth surface, and are then continued to be used until they finally burst. It is only then that they are retreaded for the first time. If they cannot be retreaded, they become carrying hods for sand, brick or mortar, the smaller bits being made into soles for sandals and shoes.

A vintage Chrysler or Cadillac that would attract an American antique-car collector is no rarity in Syria, Indonesia, or the northeastern states of Brazil. In some cases the motor has been rebuilt into a diesel engine to save fuel and the roof has been turned into a large baggage area which is bursting with squawking chickens, bolts of fabric, luggage, and agricultural tools. Usually the trunk has been greatly enlarged and the car often carries twelve to fifteen passengers, operating at thirty miles an hour as an economy class, cross-country taxi.

Virtually no American or European mechanic could match the

Figure 8-11. *Paraffin lamp made from a recycled light bulb, a soft drink bottlecap and a wick. These lamps are made and used by the thousands by the poor nordestinos of Brazil. First brought to my attention by João Grijó and Claudia Brandão Mattos of Rio de Janeiro. (Author's collection)*

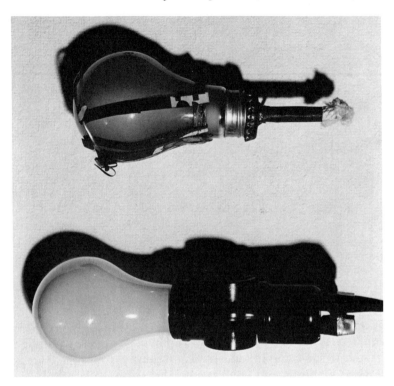

innovative ability and skill of his Oriental counterpart. Trained only to replace or repair parts that allegedly no longer perform, he could never compete with people who smooth out crushed body parts and carefully straighten and rechrome bent bumpers and window frames. Spare parts that are no longer available are routinely carved and filed out of raw metal blocks. In Bombay, thirty-five-year-old, three-wheel taxis (figures 8-12 and 8-13) dart in and out of heavy pedestrian and vehicular traffic on incredibly poor road surfaces and some of the engines have been in use for over a million miles.

All of these examples have had a powerful impact on the young

Figure 8-12. *Three-wheeled taxi-cum-truck from Bombay.*

designers visiting the third world. Hundreds of books, pamphlets, magazine articles, and broadcasts continuously exhort us to return to a more balanced and environmentally responsible life. But to most western students (most westerners, in fact), it's all theory—dead stuff. It is necessary to live and work in the third world to understand how it can be achieved. "Recycling" cannot be translated into most native dialects. Everything is used frugally, maintained carefully, repaired painstakingly, and, when it is no longer useful in its original form, it is melted down and hammered into a different shape and reused.

Figure 8-13. *Detail of the steering column.*

Conclusion

THROUGHOUT history, cross-fertilization between differing cultures has enriched the fabric of society. The drab and homogenous society of medieval times was transformed into a splendid tapestry of architecture, music, and the fine arts through the Renaissance. The rediscovery of Greek and Roman civilization and Marco Polo's travels to Cathay added intellectual as well as aromatic spice to life in Italy. What we are learning from Japan (and to a lesser extent from India and China Islamic countries) is providing another intellectual and aesthetic platform from which to leap into a future rich with options.

At times it still seems as if the mass media, the predominant international style in architecture and design, electronic communication and consumer addiction fanned by advertisers, is giving us a homogenous, undifferentiated world society—not a global village, but a global housing development.

If we are to avoid this, we must recognize that there are still highly separate views of the world from which we can learn. In discussing the work done with and for third world countries, we can see that for a truly mature and cooperative relationship we are on a two-way street—there is much that we can teach, but more that we can learn. The necessity for survival has made those who live in the southern hemisphere marvelously innovative and imaginative. Unfortunately, this may be a talent we have lost.

In the mid-1950s, designers visiting the third world would sweep into a native region like white missionaries, forcing their wisdom on the natives. It took them years to learn that these people need half horsepower tractors more than large combines; sanitary latrines more than intensive care units for the elderly; simple teaching devices more than expensive electronic audiovisual entertainment; improved roads more than 747s. Their hopes lie so close to sheer survival, their needs are so different from ours that it is difficult to build bridges of understanding.

It is the role of designers to search the past for better alternatives to modern methods, and to examine how other people are solving the same problems that beset us. All good design is *appropriate.* Any product should be appropriate to the task it performs, the people that use it, and the materials from which it is made. It must also be appropriate to the tools and processes that will produce it, to our sense of ethics, and to life in an energy-starved world and to the environment.

There are so many groups from which we can learn. We have already seen part of what the third world can teach us. But there are also babies and small children who look at the world through fresh eyes; the physically and mentally handicapped who depend on our ingenuity to help them lead fruitful lives; industrial workers and farmers whose lives are a mixture of peril, monotony, and hard labor; and women encumbered by sexist stereotypes. These and other groups all have in common that their lives are made challenging by being at odds with the mainstream. Architects and designers can learn from these groups to all of our profit. But they can only achieve this by working with them. The road to a better future is a two-way street.

Chapter Notes

Introduction

1. *The Oxford Unabridged Dictionary of the English Language.* Oxford: The Clarendon Press, 1970.
2. *Kansas City Star,* October 10, 1979.
3. From the Opening Speech at the Exhibition by Franco Pinelli, International Design Centre, Berlin, September 1981.
4. A listing of these books and articles would run to many pages. I would suggest my own: *How Things Don't Work,* Papanek and Hennessey (57),* as well as the extensive bibliography contained in that book.
5. Papanek (55).
6. Dwight Packer: "Utilizing Biological Principles in Design," University of Kansas, 1981 (unpublished).

Chapter 1

1. Kamal Jumblat was a statesman, patriot, and poet who served as Minister of the Interior in Lebanon until his assassination in 1977. See Jumblat (32).

---

* Numbers in parentheses refer to Bibliography.

Chapter 2

1. This slogan was first used by me as the introductory quote to a chapter "Die Aussicht von Heute" (Design: The View From Today), which appeared as a chapter in: *Design ist Unsichtbar (Design is Invisible)*, Papanek (53). It has been marked only because a similar quote was used by a student group of mine in Brazil in 1980.
2. This incredible statement was made to me in 1978 by a nurse/ therapist working in a retirement home for the elderly and associated with the Public Health Service of Missouri. Her two colleagues, employed in the same nursing home, nodded and smiled in complete agreement with her.
3. The children were shown simple sketched models and drawings. Textile samples and pieces of wood and metal were actually handled by them. They were exposed to different color choices and asked to commit themselves to these.
4. Papanek and Hennessey (57), especially Chapter Four.
5. Roger Dalton: *Safety by Design*, his thesis done under the direction of the author in postgraduate Industrial Design (Engineering) at the Manchester Polytechnic Institute in England, 1975.

Chapter 3

1. This advertisement is typical of the marketing approach to the public practiced by the American automobile industry. It appeared as a double-page, four-color advertisement in *Time* (U.S. Edition), October 10, 1977.

   Since then the ever-shrinking market for American automobiles has changed the main thrust of advertisement, but not their ma- nipulative intent. As this is being written, *Newsweek* (March 30, 1981), makes it possible to compare Japanese vs. U.S. approaches. Ford (with its slowly aging "better idea"), uses a two-color, double- page spread on the *Cougar* under the headings: *"Sports Cat"* and *"Class Cat."* There is much about the car's *"classic profile and sporty styling"*, its *"Sporty Recarro Seats"* and a *"Keyless Entry System."* The copywriter then goes into ecstasies over the *"Convertible-Look Carriage Roof"* (sic). The *"Class Cat"* ad talks about *"Luxury, Elegant Space and Tailored Appointments"* like *"The Optional Twin Comfort Lounge Seats"*. It also brags about a *"leather-wrapped steering wheel"*; this last option is available from any auto supply store for $4.97.

   By comparison, Datsun under the headline *"Blueprint for Quality"* uses the key phrase: *"More miles per gallon. More years per car"*. The

Datsun ad talks about very specific welding techniques, rust protection, antichipping compounds and engine redesign, gas-saving, durability of the car, safety, and maintenance.
2. *U.S. News and World Report*, November 12, 1980.
3. Toffler (73).
4. Papanek (57), pp. 23*ff*.

Chapter 4

1. Mark Brutton, former editor, *Design* (Great Britain) in a lecture delivered at the Kansas City Art Institute, 1978.
2. *Ibid.*
3. Comment from the marketing manager of a large discount high-fidelity chain in the United States, 1980.
4. I carried out these experiments between 1954 and 1980 with students in their first semester of their first year of design studies, as well as with graduate students. These experiments were done at the Ontario College of Art (Toronto, Canada), the State University of New York at Buffalo, the Rhode Island School of Design, the School of Design of North Carolina State College at Raleigh, Purdue University, the California Institute of the Arts, the Royal Academy of Architecture of Denmark (Copenhagen), the Architectural Association (London, England), Carleton University (Ottawa, Canada), and the Kansas City Art Institute.

Chapter 5

1. Lock (44), printed and distributed through the good offices of the Royal Academy of Architecture (Copenhagen), 1973.

Chapter 6

1. These books are among the most interesting dealing with decentralization from the viewpoint of an architect or designer in the Bibliography. To these should be added: Baer (3), Blake (5), Douglas (12), Dubos (14), Ellul (18), Fathy (20), Fritsch (24), Harris (31), Kohr (37), Kohr (38), Kohr (39), Lovelock (46), Morgan (51), McRobie (52), Rifkin (62), Schumacher (64), Thurow (71), and Todd (72).
2. Martin Pawley: *The Private Future*, London: Thames & Hudson, 1973.
3. Frank Lloyd Wright first wrote about his concept of Broadacre City in *The Disappearing City*, just as work on the large-scale models of

Broadacre City began at Taliesin West. His clearest philosophical statement on the city plan was published under the title *The New Frontier: Broadacre City*. He added further drawn and written material, all this appeared as *When Democracy Builds*. His final statements appear in *The Living City*. See Wright (80–83).

4. On the question of "graphic Esperanto," there is really no such thing. However the question of *Isotype* (an attempt to communicate graphically across cultural lines, first invented in Austria), is best discussed in the magazine *Icographic*, a scholarly journal published by Patrick Wallis Burke in England. See issues 5, 6, 9, 11, and 12, and especially 8 and 10.

Chapter 7

1. Wills (77). This quote is from Chapter Three: "On Liberty and Safety." Wills was the pioneer of gliding in Great Britain. His influence extended all over the world. Since I myself pilot sail planes and gliders, I have found his books fascinating and packed with practical lore. Of wider interest is his writing on risk-taking and the eternal clash between individualism and the mass—liberty and safety. See also Wills (78–79).

2. *"Bisociation" Technique* was developed by me as a problem solving tool in the early 1960s. The name derives from bi-association: the forceful collision between two opposite ideas. This has been lucidly and intelligently discussed by Arthur Koestler in his seminal book *The Act of Creation* (34). Koestler describes the result of these collisions in humor, scientific discovery, and peak religious experiences as the *"Ha Ha," "Ha!"* and *"Ah . . ."* reactions, respectively. The word bi-association was first coined by Arthur Koestler in *Insight & Outlook*, his earlier book on the creative process. *Trisociation* is here presented for the first time.

   It is possible to systematically engineer these collisions, the result will be a new insight in problem solving, frequently a new discovery. I have described this method in my forthcoming book *By Accident or Design?* as well as on my PBS radio design commentary of the same title.

Chapter 8

1. René Dubos seems to have originated the phrase "Think globally, act locally." At the Dubos Forum at Corvallis, Oregon in June, 1980, he agreed with me to amend it as given at the chapter heading,

to help divert architects and designers from the seductiveness of the grandiose.

2. Eysenck (19).
3. *Ibid.*
4. Thorpe (70).
5. Quoted by Koestler (34).
6. See also: William Katavolos: *Organics*, Hilversum, Holland: De Jong & Co., 1961.
7. Lorenz (45).

Bibliography

Many of these books deal with "appropriate", "alternative", or "intermediate technology." During the last nine or ten years quite a bit has been published that deals with small scale and appropriate size. But the relationship between human scale on one hand and architecture and design on the other has not been fully examined in any book. Listed below are some of the books that have helped me in my research and refreshed me through their authors' having come to parallel conclusions in other fields.

1. Christopher Alexander, *The Linz Café/Das Linz Cafe*, New York: Oxford University Press, 1981.

2. Michael Allaby, *Inventing Tomorrow*, London: Abacus, 1976.

3. Steve Baer, *Sunspots: An Exploration of Solar Energy*, Seattle: Cloudburst Press, 1979.

4. Gregory Bateson, *Mind and Nature: A Necessary Unity*, New York: E. P. Dutton, 1979.

5. Peter Blake, *Form Follows Fiasco*, Boston: Atlantic, Little, Brown, 1977.

6. John Brooks, *Showing Off in America*, Boston: Little, Brown & Co., 1981.

7. Abner Cohen, *Two-Dimensional Man: An Essay on the Anthropology of Power and Symbolism in Complex Society*, London: Routledge & Kegan Paul Ltd., 1974.

8. Alex Comfort, *Art and Social Responsibility*, London: Falcon Press, 1946.

9. Theodore Andrea Cook, *The Curves of Life*, London: Constable & Co., 1940.

10. Jerome Deshusses, *The Eighth Night of Creation*, New York: Dial Press, 1982.

11. György Doczi, *The Power of Limits: Proportional Harmonies in Nature, Art & Architecture*, Boulder, Colorado: Shambhala Publications, 1981.

12. Mary Douglas, *The World of Goods*, New York: Basic Books, 1979.

13. René Dubos, *Celebrations of Life*, New York: McGraw-Hill, 1980.

14. ———, *The Wooing of Earth*, New York: Charles Scribner's Sons, 1980.

15. Duane Elgin, *Voluntary Simplicity*, New York: William Morrow, 1981.

16. Willis D. Ellis, *A Source Book of Gestalt Psychology*, London: Routledge & Kegan Paul Ltd., 1938.

17. Jacques Ellul, *The Technological System*, New York: Continuum, 1980.
18. ————, *Trahison de l'Occident*, Paris: Calmann-Levy, 1975. (Also available in a translation by Matthew J. O'Connell as *The Betrayal of the West*, New York: Seabury Press, 1978.)
19. H. J. Eysenck, *Sense and Nonsense in Psychology*, Middlesex: Pelican Books, 1968.
20. Hassan Fathy, *Architecture for the Poor*, Chicago: University of Chicago Press, 1973.
21. Paulo Freire, *Cultural Action for Freedom*, Middlesex: Penguin, 1972.
22. ————, *Educacão como Prática da Liberdade*, São Paulo: P.P.C., 1967.
23. ————, *Pedagogy of the Oppressed*, Middlesex: Penguin, 1972.
24. Bruno Fritsch, *Die Vierte Welt: Modell einer neuen Wirklichkeit*, Stuttgart DVA, 1970.
25. Irving J. Gantrall, *The Ecology of the Orthoptera and Dermaptera of the George Reserve in Michigan*, University of Michigan Press, 1943.
26. E. H. Gombrich, *Art and Illusion: A Study in the Psychology of Pictorial Representation*, Princeton: Bollingen, 1961.
27. ————, *Ideals and Idols: Essays on Values in History and in Art*, Oxford: Phaidon Press Ltd., 1979.
28. ————, *The Sense of Order: A Study in the Psychology of Decorative Art*, Oxford: Phaidon Press Ltd., 1979.
29. Paul Goodman, *Art and Social Nature*, New York: Vinco Publishing, 1946.
30. Herb Greene, *Mind & Image: An Essay on Art & Architecture*, Lexington, Kentucky: The University Press of Kentucky, 1976.
31. Marvin Harris, *Cultural Materialism: The Struggle for a Science of Culture*, New York: Random House, 1979.
32. Kamal Jumblat, *The Man and His Struggle*, Lebanon: Information Committee for Jumblat's International Day on May 1st, 1977.
33. David Katz, *Gestalt Psychology: Its Nature and Significance*, New York: The Ronald Press, 1950.
34. Arthur Koestler, *The Act of Creation*, New York: Macmillan, 1964.
35. ————, *Bricks to Babel*, London: Hutchinson & Co. Ltd., 1980.
36. ————, *Janus: A Summing Up*, London: Hutchinson & Co. Ltd., 1978.
37. Leopold Kohr, *The Breakdown of Nations*, London: Routledge & Kegan Paul Ltd., 1957.
38. ————, *Development Without Aid*, London: Christopher Davies, 1973.
39. ————, *The Over-Developed Nations*, New York: Schocken Books, 1977.

40.   Satish Kumar (ed.), *The Schumacher Lectures*, London: Blond & Briggs, 1980.
41.   W. R. Lethaby, *A Continuing Presence: Essays from Form in Civilization*, Manchester, England: British Thornton Ltd., 1982.
42.   ———, *Architecture, Mysticism and Myth*, New York: George Braziller, 1975.
43.   ———, *Architecture, Nature & Magic*, New York: George Braziller, 1956.
44.   Christine Lock, *Some Notes & Suggestions on Hand-Milling & Making Hand Mills*, Copenhagen: Royal Academy of Architecture, 1973.
45.   Konrad Lorenz, *Über Tierisches und Menschliches Verhalten*, Munich, Germany: Piper, 1966.
46.   J. E. Lovelock, *Gaia: A New Look at Life on Earth*, Oxford: Oxford University Press, 1979.
47.   Amory B. Lovins, *Soft Energy Paths*, New York: Harper & Row, 1979.
48.   Thomas Mann, *Confessions of Felix Krull, Confidence Man*, New York: Knopf, 1955.
49.   Peter Medawar and Julian Shelley (eds.), *Structure in Science and Art*, Amsterdam: Excerpta Medica, 1980.
50.   Henry Miller, *My Bike & Other Friends*, Santa Barbara, California: Capra Press, 1978.
51.   Chris Morgan, *Future Man?*, London: David & Charles, 1980.
52.   George McRobie, *Small is Possible*, New York: Harper & Row, 1981.
53.   Victor Papanek, "Die Aussicht von Heute" ("The View From Today") in *Design ist Unsichtbar* (*Design is Invisible*), Vienna, Austria: Löcker Verlag, 1981.
54.   ———, *"Big Character" Poster No. 1: Work Chart for Designers*, Charlottenlund, Denmark, 1973.
55.   ———, *Design for the Real World*, New York: Pantheon Books, 1971.
56.   ———, "Socio-Environmental Consequences of Design" in *Health & Industrial Growth*, Holland: Associated Scientific Publishers, 1975, (CIBA Symposium XXII).
57.   Victor Papanek and James Hennessey, *How Things Don't Work*, New York: Pantheon Books, 1977.
58.   Felix R. Paturi, *Nature, Mother of Invention: The Engineering of Plant Life*, Middlesex: Pelican, 1978.
59.   Peter and Susan Pearce, *Experiments in Form*, New York: Van Nostrand Reinhold, 1978.

60. ———, *Polyhedra Primer*, New York: Van Nostrand Reinhold, 1978.

61. Ian Rawlins, *Aesthetics and the Gestalt*, London: Nelson, 1953.

62. Jeremy Rifkin, *Entropy*, New York: Viking Press, 1980.

63. Marshall Sahlins, *Stone Age Economics*, London: Tavistock, 1974.

64. E. F. Schumacher, *Good Work*, New York: Harper & Row, 1979.

65. *Shield-Backed Katydids*, Philadelphia: Memoirs of the American Entomological Society, Vol. 29, 1973.

66. Aleksandr I. Solzhenitsyn, *A World Split Apart*, New York: Harper & Row, 1978.

67. L. S. Stavrianos, *Global Rift: The Third World Comes of Age*, New York: William Morrow & Co., 1981.

68. ———, *The Promise of the Coming Dark Age*, San Francisco: W. H. Freeman & Co., 1976.

69. Peter S. Stevens, *Patterns in Nature*, Boston: Little, Brown, 1974.

70. W. H. Thorpe, *Science, Man and Morals*, London: Scientific Book Club, 1966.

71. Lester C. Thurow, *The Zero-Sum Society*, New York: Basic Books, 1980.

72. John and Nancy Todd, *Tomorrow is Our Permanent Address*, New York: Harper & Row, 1980.

73. Alvin Toffler, *Future Shock*, New York: Random House, 1970.

74. ———, *The Third Wave*, New York: Morrow, 1980.

75. John F. C. Turner, *Housing by People: Towards Autonomy in Building Environments*, London: Marion Boyars Ltd., 1976.

76. David Watkin, *Morality and Architecture*, Oxford: Clarendon Press, 1977.

77. Philip Wills, *Free as a Bird*, London: John Murray Publishers Ltd., 1973.

78. ———, *On Being a Bird*, London: David & Charles, 1977.

79. ———, *Where No Birds Fly*, London: Newnes Ltd., 1961.

80. Frank Lloyd Wright, *The Disappearing City*, New York: William Farquhar Payson, 1932.

81. ———, *The Living City*, New York: Horizon Press, 1958.

82. ———, *The New Frontier: Broadacre City*, Springreen, Wisconsin: Taliesin Fellowship Publication, Volume 1, Number 1, October, 1940.

83. ———, *When Democracy Builds*, Chicago: Chicago University Press, 1945.

84. Sōetsu Yanagi, *The Unknown Craftsman: A Japanese Insight into Beauty*, Tokyo: Kodansha International, 1972.

85. Knut Yran, *A Joy Forever*, Melbourne: Industrial Design Institute of Australia, 1980.

Index

Page numbers in italic refer to illustrations.